PERMISSION
to party

*

taking
time to
celebrate
and
enjoy life

Jill Murphy Long

SOURCEBOOKS, INC.®
NAPERVILLE, ILLINOIS

Library of Congress Cataloging-in-Publication Data

Long, Jill Murphy.
  Permission to party : taking time to celebrate and enjoy life / by Jill Murphy Long.
     p. cm.
  ISBN 1-4022-0198-2 (alk. paper)
  1. Entertaining. 2. Parties. 3. Cookery. I. Title.
TX731.L5774 2004
642'.4—dc22
                              2003027650

Published by Sourcebooks, Inc.
P.O. Box 4410, Naperville, Illinois 60567-4410
(630) 961-3900
FAX: (630) 961-2168
www.sourcebooks.com

ISBN 1-4022-0198-2

Printed and bound in the United States of America
ED 10 9 8 7 6 5 4 3 2 1

Other books by Jill Murphy Long

Permission to Nap: Taking Time to Restore Your Spirit
Permission to Play: Taking Time to Renew Your Smile

To Greg and Brittany—May you always find life a party!

Acknowledgments

Without my support team, this book would still remain a distant dream. Many thanks for the hours of encouragement from those who helped, in their own insightful ways: Greg and Brittany Long; my dad, Bill Murphy; my sister, Amy Murphy; and my brother, Mike Murphy; my editor, Deb Werksman, and my literary agent, Elizabeth Pomada; my publicist, Barbi Pecenco, and her associates; the sales and marketing force at Sourcebooks, including Bob Olson and Sean Murray; and my publisher, Dominique Raccah.

Special thanks to reference librarian Alysa Selby of the Bud Werner Memorial Library for her incredible research and Karen Fitzgerald for her speedy deliveries of all my interlibrary loans. Oftentimes during the writing of this book, my house looked like an adjunct of the public library.

Thank you to Leslie and Dick Ryan at *Off the Beaten Path,* who reserved a writing table and chair for me each and every day of the year (I needed this second office to complete this manuscript as well as my previous books). Thank you to all of the booksellers across the country that continue to recommend my books every day, especially the independent bookstores, teahouses, and gift shops.

Thanks also to all of the spas that have embraced the philosophy penned within the pages of the *Permission to...* book series, including but not limited to: Sol Day Spa of Steamboat Springs; Spa Gregories of Newport Beach, California; and The Golden Door Spa.

Once again, I want to thank all of my readers and the reading groups who have welcomed my ideas, suggestions, and books into their circles, in particular the Rancho Book Club of California—Jan Schlieder and all of her avid and enthusiastic readers. With your ongoing support, I can and will continue to write many more books in this series. Thank you for allowing me to explore this wonderful journey as an author. May you find permission to do whatever you dream of doing. *Cheers!*

Table of Contents

introduction

Welcome to the wonderful world of celebrations—where indulgences are permitted regularly and parties can be both grand and simple. Based on the premise of, "It is the thought that counts," this party book provides numerous new ways to say, "Thank you," "Happy Birthday!" and "Congratulations!" With as many party themes, tips, recipe shortcuts, and time-saving ideas tucked in this book as there are days in a year, your toughest decision will be what type of party to plan first.

Permission to Party is all about developing a gratitude for life—sharing time together, conversation, hearty laughs, and of course, good food to help us slow down and love and treasure every day, not just the milestones of life. I wrote *Permission to Party*, a book about celebrating, food, and eating, to help women indulge without guilt.

Many envy the French lifestyle, which is often referred to as the French paradox. They drink wine, eat cheese, cook with real butter and fresh whole milk, savor gourmet foods, eat desserts daily, and suffer no problem with their weight.

Perhaps it is their expression, *joie de vivre,* or "the joy of living," that has them viewing the world as a party to be celebrated every day.

In a nationwide survey, American women tallied a depressingly low number of parties hosted and attended, and many considered most of these dates mandatory—"We celebrate my birthday because my family wants to, not me."

On my book tours, I listened as women told me their personal family traditions and unique ways to celebrate. They also shared their thoughts about comfort foods and retro foods. I watched as their eyes shone when they savored an imaginary bite of their favorite— yet forbidden and seldom-savored—foods.

These findings revealed the American woman's unspoken guilt surrounding the act of eating; her frustrations about the paraded "ideal body" for all; and confusion about por- tion size, carbohydrates, sugars, fats, and which diet, if any, works. However, the bright side of these candid talks and handwritten notes was the women who are happy with their bodies and their eating habits. Their self-acceptance and newfound peace is shared throughout this book.

While *Permission to Party* is written to assist you in handling a crowd or the family at the holidays again, it is also about having a party for you. Ideas and suggestions will help you establish a personal ritual to honor the person you are today and who you are becoming with each passing year. This time spent alone in celebration of you is another good rea- son to celebrate life and a very good way to recharge your mind and body.

If we adopt our French sisters' philosophy as our own, perhaps we can learn to enjoy our birthday party, another Monday-morning breakfast, and the "every days" in our lives more often and more fully.

I also wrote this book for those who don't or cannot cook, but would love to throw a party. Martha Stewart I am not. In fact, the only class I ever flunked was Home Econom- ics in junior high school. (Afterward I petitioned for girls to be allowed into wood and metal shop—and won.)

I tell you this story because, while this is a party book filled with historical food notes, ideas to start a family baking or cooking tradition, international appetizer recipes, and how to host an all-American celebration any time of the year, it is especially for those not born with a cooking gene.

From Costa Rica to Washington, D.C., to Portland, Oregon, women mailed, faxed, and emailed great nonalcoholic beverage suggestions, easy appetizer tips, and tasty recipes that even I, the Home-Ec flunky, could handle with finesse.

This literary trek through foreign kitchens and open-air markets of the world will encourage hesitant cooks and party hostesses to combine familiar ingredients with new to create a brand-new meal, centerpiece, or party.

For those who wish to host a gathering, but are at a loss as to what type of celebration to plan, intercontinental party themes and ideas are offered from India, Denmark, Italy, Great Britain, China, and the United States. See how the world celebrates its traditions, holidays, birthdays, and name days, and borrow a new idea for your next feast.

When our eyes are opened to how other chefs, cooks, and busy women throughout the world handle the three-times-a-day event of meal preparation (as well as grand occasions), the courage and means to try something original will be found. Be inspired by the advice and tips of true culinary masters and kitchen icons. Apply the suggested time-management strategies and the shortcuts in the kitchen, ask for help, and watch how your life becomes a party—an exclamation of living well—each and every day.

Parties are meant to be enjoyed not only by the guest, but by the hostess, too. Gather your truest friends frequently for any excuse to celebrate life. Enter this gastronomical world and emerge on the other side—full of life.

Here's to your health, your happiness, and your life!

chapter 1

women who celebrate WHOLEHEARTEDLY

*and without permission

> To enjoy the flavor of life, take big bites.
> —Robert Heinlein (1907–1988)

The history of eating and celebrating starts in ancient Rome, with lavish feasts lasting as long as ten hours. Such banquets came to be described as *ab ovo usque ad mala* (from eggs to apples) and included such delicacies as seafood, flamingo, heron, camel's feet, and perhaps a centerpiece dish of roasted larks inside a duck inside a peacock, followed by dessert trays of fruits and fancy sweets. Acrobats and fire-eaters entertained the guests. Hosts and their cooks competed to create the most exotic dishes, and the opulent meals became ever larger and longer.

The concept of reclining on couches to dine began in Greece around 700 BC and was adopted by the Romans. Each couch (sometimes shared by two people) had a low table alongside to hold the food, and special rooms—the predecessors of our dining rooms—were built to accommodate sometimes more than one hundred.

During the Middle Ages, gluttony was popular, with pauses for entertainment between excesses of food and drink. In 1237, at the marriage of Robert, Comte d'Artois, one interlude featured a horseman crossing a rope above the heads of the guests. Musicians circled the banquet tables seated upon oxen to play, and monkeys scampered around waving their harps. Whether or not they played the instruments well was not noted in the record of the feast.

Heliogabalus, an emperor from Syria, never ate an inexpensive meal, never drank twice from the same goblet (fashioned from either pure silver or gold), and had his party napkins painted, of course, in gold.

Some weddings are known to have erred on the side of grandiosity. In London in 1243, to celebrate the exchange of nuptial vows between Richard, Earl of Cornwall (brother of Henry III brother), and Sanchia, the Comte de Provence's daughter, more than thirty thousand dishes were presented for the marriage banquet.

Feast or Famine

Over the later centuries and around the world, women have endured all types of notions in the name of beauty and cultural acceptance revolving around food and their bodies.

In the sixteenth century, iron corsets gave Catherine de Médici, Queen of France, her much desired and envied thirteen-inch waist. With tightly pulled corsets and scarce amounts of food consumed, she fainted daily. In opulent living rooms across Europe, "fainting couches" were as prevalent then as our big-screen televisions are today.

Later, women gave up the struggle to achieve an ideal waist size and decided beauty was worth carrying around an extra fifteen pounds from the weight of petticoats and voluminous whalebone hoop skirts. Crinolines, a danger to any woman who wore them, could become entangled in the wheels of a passing carriage, could upset the wearer in high winds, and were highly flammable.

After the French Revolution, women dispensed with the corsets, an artifact of the aristocracy, and fancied the sheer empire dress with its high (and nonrestrictive) waistline. Since comfort was the mantra of those days, these women celebrated wholeheartedly and without permission, but surely those pleasures were short-lived.

At the end of the nineteenth century in America, the Gibson Girl, originally created as an illustration, set a new standard of beauty: be tall (difficult for the petite), be graceful, and be athletic. The roaring twenties promptly replaced this approved body type with a boyish figure, sans breasts, for all women. After World War I, the girdle arrived with an uncanny similarity to the previous centuries' corset, and once more it was difficult and uncomfortable to enjoy good food at a party, let alone get proper nourishment.

> Everything I like is either illegal, immoral, or fattening.
> —Alexander Woollcott
> (1887–1943)

The problem with these prescriptions of the past remained the fact that women were impaired in almost all everyday activities: standing, walking, thinking, and even eating.

Today—with approximately 70 percent of American women on a diet at any given time, the popularity of high-heeled shoes and Wonderbras, and the readily available options of liposuction and plastic surgery—has much changed?

Permission to Celebrate

To eat, the simple act of nourishing the body, has become so complicated, so confusing, so forbidden that we have forgotten that the purpose of this daily motion is to fuel the body, the mind, and the spirit.

In my nationwide survey, I searched to find what the American woman did or did not celebrate, how she felt about hosting parties, daily meal preparation, eating, and food.

According to a survey by *People* magazine in 2000, only 10 percent of the women surveyed were completely satisfied with their bodies—even the women who appeared to have near-perfect bodies found something they disliked...stomachs, hips, butt, arms, breast size. The survey also revealed that many had had plastic surgery or were considering it and would try a diet even if it posed a slight health risk.

The study's responses revealed what has been supported regularly by the advertisements found in national magazines: a discord between body image and body reality, which greatly impacts a woman's ability to enjoy a party and sometimes, life.

Guilt, not pleasure, is associated with eating and celebrating in the United States. In a word-association study, French women chose the word *celebrate* to match *cake*; American women selected the word *guilt*.

Present a party invitation and many women stress. Some report declining social activities where skin is bared, especially poolside and beach activities. Still others eat before going out to dinner, so as not to be seen eating in public. Instead of anticipating a graduation, an upcoming wedding, or a retirement party, many women agonize over "How to avoid so much food?" and "What can I wear that still fits me?" Or worse yet, they begin a drastic diet, only to gain more weight afterward than if they had simply indulged a bit at the party.

Permission needs to be granted to celebrate our milestones, traditions, and individual moments, all of which make our lives fulfilling and worthwhile. Until we learn to dismiss America's recommendation of the ideal female body dished up daily by the media and Hollywood, we will never truly enjoy a party. A gala, a bash, a festival, or a carnival is about good food, good friends, and good conversation. If we are anxious over the first ingredient of a fine celebration, how are we ever going to enjoy the rest?

Since 1958, Mattel's Barbie doll continues to perpetuate the myth of the perfect American woman with measurements of 39-23-33.

"I Am Happy with My Body." True or False?

Women can be their own harshest critics, full of self-reproach and self-hatred, fueled by the ceaseless ammunition they hear, see, and read every single day. This constant comparison of the ideal female body verses actual shape and size can prove paralyzing.

Dr. Barbara Levy, a Seattle gynecologist and cofounder of the Real Woman Project, a resource center for self-esteem improvement, says the average American woman is about 5' 4" and weighs about 152 pounds. In July 2002, *Good Housekeeping* magazine reported that the average female model in America is 5' 11" and weighs 115 pounds.

No wonder there is a huge discrepancy between reality and fantasy when we look in the mirror.

Impossible Role Models

Beginning in the 1950s, health experts noted an increase in the contemporary woman's desire for thinness. In the sixties, seventeen-year-old British model Lesley Hornby, called "Twiggy" due to her twig-like shape, became the model cast for mannequins and the ideal for many women and girls.

Ever since Twiggy took center stage on fashion's catwalk in 1967, the mantra heard on Hollywood's filming lots has been, "Thin is in." Unfortunately, at 31-23-32 and ninety pounds, this starved look embraced by women and men alike and endorsed by the mass media had a devastating effect on the physical and mental health of women for decades after her debut.

Anyone who thinks that society pressures women to live up to our image should think of what we have to go through to maintain that image.
—*Carol Alt (b. 1960)*

Unattainable Results

Over the years, the bodies of models have become thinner and the number of diet articles larger. Both of these recurring images and messages broadcast throughout society helps the diet industry get richer at the expense of women's body dissatisfaction and makes it increasingly difficult to enjoy a good party with good food. The guilt and shame of overeating or the hostility of not eating does not make for a good party temperament.

Body acceptance, of all sizes and shapes for women and by women, needs to start with each one of us. When we refuse to buy into the prescribed norm, a difference is felt, a ripple goes out across the shopping malls, restaurants, and grocery stores to let those body-mold makers know what we will stand for—in particular, what we will and will not buy.

> In 1993, bone-baring, 5' 10" size six super-model Kate Dillon was asked to lose twenty pounds in order to continue working in the industry. She asked, "From where?"

Reality Check

Cosmetic surgery is *de rigueur* in Hollywood, yet in America there is a refreshing wave rising against Hollywood's fat phobia and the celebrities who endorse this unrealistic ideal of what American women should weigh and what size they should wear.

Celebrities such as Kate Winslet, Jennifer Lopez, Andie MacDowell, Cindy Crawford, Minnie Driver, and Catherine Zeta-Jones have taken a stand against society's expected size for grown women. They have permitted their bodies to be the shape and size they are in accordance with their bone structure and genes and with regard to good health. What a relief!

> ...it is sad to me that too many women look outside themselves to others to improve their lives rather than looking inward.
> —Camryn Manheim (b. 1961)

Model Emme, who has made a career of modeling her two hundred–pound figure and is the host of E! Entertainment Television's *Fashion Emergency*, says: "It takes a lot of work for us not to buy into a fifty-billion-dollar diet-related industry. If we start saying, 'I want to be happy with myself and whatever shape I was given at birth,' I think it's going to change [people's perception about the ideal size for women]."

> *Mode*, the fashion magazine written for plus-sized women, reports 30 percent of North American women wear a size fourteen or larger.

Multimedia extraordinaire Oprah Winfrey has shown women that weight does not have to matter in the game of success. "Oprah is someone who transcends her weight," says Andrienne Ressler, body-image specialist.

> **Sandra Bullock, who gained fifteen pounds for the movie *Speed*, said, "I'm never going to be thin and waif-like. I tried; it's not going to work. I love my body now that it's softer."**

"Healthier" is what happens when actresses, models, and women everywhere refuse to accept the mass media's dictated ideal weight of 110 pounds for all American women.

"Happier" is what women feel when they stop listening to others about what size pants they should wear.

"Stronger" is what women become when they eat well for their minds, bodies, and spirits.

Real Models

At the 1999 women's soccer World Cup, each player's name, position, height, and weight were announced. Finally, America is seeing real role models who show off

> **My body brought these three amazing kids into the world. I'll keep it as healthy as I can, but I'm not living up to anybody else's standard but my own.**
> —*Christie Brinkley (b. 1954)*

muscle instead of ribs; healthy women who weigh a real weight and who are proud of it. I believe these women are better role models than any fashion model could ever be for young girls and for their mothers, who also saw those models in action.

In the September 2002 issue of *More* magazine, actress Jamie Lee Curtis decided to come out and end the myth of "the perfect Jamie." She bared the truth and allowed a natural photo to be taken of her without the usual three hours of hair styling and makeup application performed by a team of thirteen experts. "I want to do my part, as I develop the consciousness for it, to stop perpetuating the myth; I'm going to look the way God intends me to look…"

Celebration of Women

As author Susan Jane Gilman wrote, "To function well, women must eat well. And we must eat without shame, regret, or punishment. Eating is about many things, but it's also about power." I could not agree more.

Women need to move and act in concerted resistance. Learn and practice saying "no" to the purchase of products solely created to support the self-hatred of the body, wrinkles, and fat. We need to stop listening to the negative and unrealistic messages about what size all women should be. To move into this mindset, I suggest throwing a party.

We need to celebrate the fact that we are alive. We are amazing human beings with so much to offer. Be the catalyst and volunteer your house for this cleansing event. Instruct all women to bring their diet pills, books, and articles, any clothes waiting in the back of the closet to be worn when the magical number is reached, wrinkle cream, the bathroom scale, tape measure, and dusty exercise gadgets—anything that is not allowing them to fully live their life right now and whatever it is that is stopping them from loving themselves in this moment.

Build a bonfire and burn the paper goods. Throw away the plastic and metal items or box and donate them. Get these distracting, negative messages out of your life; remove all roadblocks once and for all and start living.

Be a friend and help a friend to see what is standing in the way of her truly knowing the wonderful woman that she already is, defined by her own standards. What a happier, healthier place this world would be if women did what was right for them! Women need to give themselves permission to love themselves now, today. Do not wait for tomorrow's reading on the bathroom scale to bring happiness and self-acceptance.

Besides, what is a party without wonderful food, and what is the point of hosting or going to a party if you cannot eat the food?

Follow your own voice. You know what is good for you and your body. The latest and best weight-loss program changes seasonally anyhow. Eat when you are hungry, celebrate more often, and sometimes even eat dessert first. Rest when you are tired, and play almost every day; then watch the word *diet* take on a new meaning in your life.

The Issue of Eating

The problem with eating in the land of plenty, however, is just that there is too much—too much on our plates, in the aisles, and available twenty-four hours every day, everywhere. As a result, junk food, diets, and unhealthy food behaviors have become an American way of life.

> **The two biggest sellers in any bookstore are the cookbooks and the diet books. The cookbooks tell you how to prepare the food, and the diet books tell you how not to eat any of it.**
> —*Andy Rooney (b. 1919)*

According to a July 2002 article in *Good Housekeeping*, the standard size six waist measurement in 1984 was twenty-three inches. By 2002 at Gap stores nationwide, a size six waist is twenty-nine inches.

Our sizes of drinks and food are larger than almost any other country in the world. Finland, by law, has a coffee break at work, but the cups are much smaller than here in the United States.

The French croissant is smaller and weighs less than its American cousin.

According to Kelly Brown, professor of psychology, epidemiology, and public health at Yale University, "One of the first things people from other countries notice when they visit the United States are the large portions served in restaurants. In most of the world, there's no such thing as a doggie bag."

A February 2002 study, published by the *American Journal of Public Health*, reported that fast-food portions have increased in recent years, an indication of what may be a major cause of obesity in the United States.

The "fat free" promises plastered on prepackaged foods don't do Americans any favors either. Now we eat the whole bag—in one sitting. When the fat is removed, the "mouth feel" is lessened. Food flavor experts assert that foods must have the right "mouth feel" in order to satisfy. Without fat, we usually eat more to compensate for this missing sensation.

Americans also drink empty but weight-adding calories with the offer of "free refills."

Order a sixty-four-ounce Big Gulp for thirty-seven cents more than the sixteen-ounce cup and take home an additional 450 calories.

Order a medium-sized buttered popcorn at the movie theater instead of a small for less than a dollar more, but get another five hundred calories and two days' worth of saturated fat.

With the advent of artificial sweeteners, we can drink more now, but also experience a diminished level of satisfaction.

Hidden Agendas

Why are the candy bars, chip bags, sodas, and every food item in the grocery stores and at the restaurants getting bigger? Where are plates for petites?

Food marketers want you to eat more of what they make. Therefore, the typical serving listed on the package is usually larger than a single portion should be, and this recommended serving has increased over the decades for a culture that has become increasingly sedentary and actually needs fewer, rather than more, calories.

In the January 2003 issue of the *Journal of the American Medical Association*, researchers at the University of North Carolina reported, "Food portions between 1977 and 1996 have increased both inside and outside the home for all categories except pizza."

As of 2003, the *Food Institute Report* noted that during 1977 to 1996, food portion sizes increased at home as well as in restaurants. The following findings may encourage you to rethink your order:

- Serving sizes of salty snacks increased from 1 ounce to 1.6 ounces, with an increase of 93 calories.
- Soft-drink sizes inflated from 13.1 fluid ounces to 19.9 ounces, adding 49 calories.
- Hamburgers expanded from 5.7 ounces to 7 ounces, for an additional 97 calories.
- Servings of french fries increased from 3.1 ounces to 3.6 ounces, adding 68 calories.
- Mexican food servings grew from 6.3 ounces to 8 ounces, packing on another 133 calories.

The conclusion of the study contrasted the daily caloric intake of Americans from 1977 to 1996, which revealed why more than 60 percent of us are overweight—the increased intake of calories each day.

According to Cecily Ann Byrne, MS, RD, at the University of Missouri–Kansas City School of Nursing, twenty years ago a typical American diet was 1,850 calories. Today, it has increased by 148 more calories a day, adding on a whopping fifteen pounds a year.

> **Never eat anything whose listed ingredients cover more than one-third of the packaging.**
> —*Joseph Goldstein Leonard (b. 1940)*

Eating Strategies

How do you counter the onslaught of the appetite-stimulating packaging of convenient, ready-to-go foods? How do you ignore those colorful bags, boxes, and bottles vying for your attention that incessantly target your immediate wants instead of your dietary needs?

Read before you serve, and make your portions appropriate for your energy requirements to feel your physical, mental, and spiritual best. Try any of these eating strategies to improve how you feel this week:

> **Facts do not cease to exist because they are ignored.**
> —*Aldous Huxley (1894–1963)*

> In 1973, the Food and Drug Administration required nutrient labeling on all foods that claim to be nutritious—no label means no nutrition.

1. Educate yourself. Read the labels and learn to decipher the nutritional facts; pay particular attention to the serving size of the package.
2. Drive past, not into, fast-food restaurants with confidence. Place your lunch box, brown paper bag, or picnic basket in the passenger seat as a deterrent so you will not fall off the wagon. Remember, you are what you eat, and today you will be another day healthier.
3. Lunch elsewhere. When time is short—no time to prepack a healthy solution—stop at a grocery store and pick up sushi, a deli sandwich sans mayo, fruit and cheese, or a premade garden salad and a crunchy baguette (and save some bread for the birds).

Eat for Your Health

A study at Rutgers University proved that commercially grown produce had substantially lower amounts of iron, manganese, calcium, and potassium. For a diet rich in nutrients, choose organic vegetables and fruits whenever the choice is offered. Be healthy in your daily choices, but still remember to celebrate with treats. When we deprive ourselves, the effort usually backfires and results in eating beyond the usual craving. Strive for balance and portion-size control, and develop a taste for healthy and natural food.

> As of October 2002, a new USDA law rules that all products displaying the word *organic* must contain at least 70 percent organic ingredients and must not have been made with any prohibited substances or practices, including: genetic engineering, irradiation, sewage sludge, or antibiotics.

Permission to Eat

This book is meant to shed a whole new light on celebrating life each day to its fullest. We need to embrace eating—food and calories—as a healthy ingredient of every day, not as a secre-

> I am not a glutton—I am an explorer of food.
> —*Erma Bombeck (1927–1996)*

tive or forbidden activity. The word *diet* as originally defined by *Webster's Dictionary*, and before Slim-Fast, means, "food and drink considered in terms of its qualities, composition, and its effect on health"—as in eating, not starving or withholding.

Balance needs to be an integral part of the American menu. Many in our society live to either one extreme or the other. We need to embrace what the French call "the golden mean" or *juste-milieu*—a point between two extremes.

Sugar Guidelines: **For a 2,200 calories-per-day diet, keep sugar intake to twelve teaspoons or forty-four grams.**

In granting yourself permission to eat, you grant love and respect for both the food and your body. You can enjoy food once again. Indulge in the art of cooking and baking. Decide to become a confident and stress-free hostess at either a small gathering or a grand celebration of life to honor a special person's milestone.

Visual Clues for the Right Portion:
3-ounce portion of protein = a deck of playing cards
½ cup of veggies or pasta = half a tennis ball
1½ ounces of cheese = six stacked dice
¼ cup of dried fruit = golf ball
1 teaspoon of butter = tip of thumb

The Promise

Pull up a kitchen chair and discover many more ways to celebrate living and eating well every day without guilt. And here is my promise: you can eat without gaining weight.

How?

- Keep your blood sugar running on an even keel throughout the day.
- Move more often.
- Eat smaller, more frequent meals, including your five or more servings of fruit and vegetables.
- Walk more often.
- Make water your new best friend and drink eight glasses a day.
- Find a form of active play that you enjoy, and do it at least five times a week. But remember, keep it fun—otherwise it won't last the summer.

When you have skipped a meal or it is close to a mealtime, avoid grocery shopping. You will probably make impulse decisions and eat too much upon returning home because you are starving. At the box chain warehouses, buy only your toilet paper and office copier paper in bulk—not prepackaged food. On the road, skip the free soda refills; don't Super-size or Big Gulp your order. At home, use a smaller plate or bowl. Fill the party table with healthy finger food made from fresh, organic ingredients. Provide activities to shake up the party crowd, and give breaks between grazing. Offer healthy snacks at eye level in the refrigerator, and limit the number of prepackaged snacks in the pantry.

This discovery of balance—the key to eating and living well—will be the end of dieting and the beginning of living.

Enjoy the Bites

Women can love life in their bodies without permission from anyone else. This acceptance of "this is my body" frees so much time and energy—and often money—previously spent on dieting, obsessing, and worrying. Going to a party should be a reason for celebration, fun, good food, and friends—not anguish. This newfound liberty to pursue life-enhancing activities is what will bring happiness, allow us to love and respect our bodies, and define who we are, not by a number, but for who we are at face value—with no excuses or apologies.

> **Everything you see I owe to spaghetti.**
> — Sophia Loren (b. 1934)

Adopt a realistic approach to your diet, not restriction or elimination, but a balance. Aim for a healthy weight, not a number on the scale. Eat to fuel your mind for productive work and creative brilliance. Eat to allow your body to move any way it craves, to dance, run, bike, or just play.

Aim for healthy eating 80 percent of the time, and the other 20 percent—celebrate! Life is meant to be lived fully, not spent counting calories. When you choose to indulge, celebrate the moment. At birthdays and weddings, have a slice of the good-luck cake. Savor the sweetness of the breakfast pastry at a neighbor's Sunday brunch or the artistic presentation of the triple-layer cake at a fine soirée.

Recent studies show that those who have dieted regain the weight and an extra five pounds or more. Do not dwell on the intake of calories or forbid the pleasure of food. Balance—be it a slice of pizza or cake—is the key to healthy, happy living. Enjoy each bite. Life is indeed too short not to be savored frequently.

Make health a priority with your eating habits and watch how your mental and physical fitness improves. You are worth it. Choose to be healthy and happiness will follow. Do something that is going to matter five years from now. It is your decision to be the woman you are. It is your life—be its author. You are worth so much more than what you weigh.

Celebrate your life! Throw a party!

> ## It is health that is real wealth, and not pieces of gold and silver.
> —*Mohandas Gandhi (1869–1948)*

> ## Eat, drink, and be merry.
> —*William Shakespeare (1564–1616)*

chapter 2

making time FOR FUN

* everyday celebrations

> **Begin each day as if it were on purpose.**
> —*Mary Anne Radmacher (b. 1957)*

Your home should be a place of sanctuary, a place where time runs according to you and not on the clock of others. Endorse a new policy of no gulping, no inhaling, and no other forms of eating on the run. If we cannot slow to enjoy what nourishes us on a daily basis, how will we stop to honor traditions and celebrate the milestones in our life?

My mantra—take time to celebrate your life—is about being here and now with our family and friends, and quiet moments with ourselves, and this includes the "everydays."

These daily moments to pause are essential—as essential as fresh air and sunshine are to our bodies. Our minds and spirits also deserve such sustenance.

The Clock of Food

During the sixteenth century, dinner was the 10 A.M. meal and supper was served at 4 P.M. One hundred years later, the dining room schedule was rearranged once again, with dinner being the meal presented at noon, followed by supper at 7 P.M.

Who sets the time for meals in your house? Maybe it is time to reclaim the hours dedicated to restoring the mind, body, and spirit with good food and good conversation. Reserve at least one meal a day to spend with others whom you care about. Send invitations if you must...

> I hope for an environment where the investigation of self will not be looked upon as self-indulgent and self-centered, but rather as self-centering. If we are not centered in self, how can we be centered in our work and our expression of human life?
> —Shirley MacLaine (b. 1934)

Time Assessment

We are all given the same twenty-four hours each day. Some of us make time work for us, and others work for the time. We all have the power to make the decisions about how to spend our time. We need to look at what can be eliminated, changed, combined, or delegated, so there is enough time for what is important in our lives. While we many not be able to do this every single day, there should be at least a few hours in every week when we can find this very important time.

The following are a few ideas on how to make time for fun and celebration in your day. First use a timer to clock how much time these activities normally take to complete. This assignment might be a real eye-opener. Then, with new

> Saying "no" can be the ultimate self-care.
> —Claudia Black (b. 1972)

time in hand, allocate it to what you know is truly important. Use a Palm Pilot, Day Planner, or wall calendar to block off time dedicated to family, food, and fun.

- *Laundry:* Forget the laundry today and see how much time immediately opens up.
- *Mail:* Skip going through the mail every day. Find a big basket, collect all the mail there, and go through it twice a week.
- *Bills*: Write out bills at the end of the week or at the month's end instead of as they arrive in the mail. Better yet, set up automatic bill paying so the bank takes care of it every month.
- *Email*: Check email only once a day, in the morning or evening. Use the block of time normally spent sitting in front of the computer to sit in front of your family and friends. Bring back the joy and comfort of good old face-to-face conversation.
- *Errands:* Pick one part of one day a week for errands. Make a list, fill bags of items for drop-off, bring empty ones for items to pick up, and plan your route to avoid driving extra miles and wasting precious minutes.
- *Household cleaning*: Clean one room a day, assign tasks, organize better storage, simplify, set a time limit to clean, or hire help. Do not let cleaning fill an entire day or weekend.
- *Cooking*: Double recipes and freeze, take out, order in, host a potluck with friends, delegate, share meal preparation, or simplify family meals.

Advice from the Breakfast Table

Always eat your breakfast. Mom was right.

Your body needs fuel (not necessarily caffeine), to "break the fast," and your brain needs carbohydrates to function. If you cannot stomach eggs, toast, and fruit before the sun rises, try to eat later,

> **All happiness depends on a leisurely breakfast.**
> —*John Gunther (1901–1970)*

around 8 or 9 A.M. Pack a hardboiled egg, a bagel, and a tropical fruit salad. Sprinkle your colorful creation with walnuts or poppy seeds, and take breakfast with you. Feed yourself right in the morning, and a healthy body and sharp mind will be your reward for the rest of the day.

In the late nineteenth century, Dr. John Harvey Kellogg, an early crusader for a simple vegetarian diet, headed the Western Health Reform Institute in Battle Creek, Michigan. His "university of health" produced the first cold breakfast cereal, the original recipe for granola, and, eventually, Corn Flakes.

Celebrate each new dawn as a blessing to be alive. Decide from today forward to begin your days with a bit of tranquility. Organize yourself the night before and guide your family to do the same. Set up a schedule, assign jobs, and create an area conducive to starting the day as an act of gratitude.

Set the breakfast table with Irish linens or hire a little one to decorate it for a shiny quarter. For the centerpiece, place a single flower in a vase. On other mornings, light an unscented candle. If someone in your family has a birthday this month, bring out the paper birthday napkins and plates early. No need to wait; acknowledge his or her happy milestone this morning. Serve birthday cake for breakfast on the special day, complete with party hats and balloons.

Sit, sip, and be glad for today. This nourishing act is meant to replenish not only the body, but the mind and spirit, too.

Caring for myself is not self-indulgence; it is self-preservation...
—Audre Lorde (1924–1992)

Same Old, Same Old

Tired of trying to get the troops—yourself included—to eat breakfast every day, let alone a healthy one? My former neighbor, Bill, made breakfast so special for his kids that other people's kids (including mine) would knock on his door. He may have been serving only pancakes, but they were buttermilk chocolate-chip pancakes.

Once a week, take an imaginary trip around the world to see what's served for the first very important meal of the day. Your crew might get excited about breakfast once again.

Breakfast Served around the World:

Caribbean: tropical fruit, eggs with hot sauce, fried plantains, vegetables, fish soup, and pastries

France: croissants, *café au lait*, and fresh fruit

Holland: bread, cheese, meat, eggs, and chocolate

Japan: sushi, miso soup, and tea

Malaysia: meat and coconut rice with curry

Middle East: yogurt, cheeses, *Souri* olives, bread dipped in olive oil and spices, bean dishes, hummus, falafel, and eggs

Spain: potato omelets, tortillas, and lots of coffee

Turkey: fresh bread or a soft pretzel with sesame called *simit*, feta cheese, green or black olives in olive oil, and Turkish tea

Kitchen aromatherapy: Try this special mixture of powdered sugar on French toast, pancakes, or waffles.
Lavender-infused Powdered Sugar
    2 tbsp. fresh lavender buds
    1 cup powdered sugar
Add the lavender buds to the powdered sugar, stir, and store in a dry, tightly capped jar. Let stand for twenty-four hours, remove buds, and then transfer sugar to a shaker jar.

Breakfast FYI: Did you know that the indentations in waffles were originally hexagons until square butter pads were introduced in 1921? The butter manufacturers must have had a lot of clout with the waffle-machine manufacturers.

Turkish coffee is served an hour after breakfast, never with breakfast.

Finland: porridge made from rye flour, rice, barley, farina, buckwheat, millet, or oatmeal with wild blueberries, lingonberries, cloudberries, black and red currants, or cran- berries, or *viili,* yogurt made of sour milk with berries

When my family tires of toast and cereal, we experiment with a few new twists on old familiar mainstays. Borrow from my fam- ily's favorites or design your own:

Fast Breakfast Sandwiches:

Breakfast Bagel: Scramble eggs with cheese and diced ham or a sausage patty, and top with a tomato slice and lettuce.

Breakfast FYI: Did you know that the word bagel is German in origin and means twisted or curved bracelet or ring?

More Kitchen Aromatherapy:
Vanilla-scented Sugar
   1 vanilla bean stick
   1 cup raw sugar
Bury the stick underneath the sugar in a jar with a tight lid. Let stand for a day. Transfer to your sugar bowl and allow the vanilla bean to remain. Use to sweeten coffee or tea, for baking, or for any recipe that calls for sugar.

Mexican Pizza: On a corn tortilla, add refried beans, cheese, and sliced Gordal olives. Heat, then top with a layer of shredded lettuce and dot with spicy salsa.

Pizza: Have any leftover slices from last night's dinner? Call it breakfast. If not, make a minipizza on a bagel or French bread with your choice of toppings.

Pita: Stuff with eggs, bacon, diced tomatoes, black Mission olives, sausage, and cheese; or for the younger palates around the table, make it a peanut-butter-and-jelly pita sandwich.

BLT: Make the usual lunch sandwich for breakfast, or any other version of this comfort food: BLA (bacon, lettuce, avocado), BTO (bacon, tomato, onion), BLTAOC (bacon, lettuce, tomato, avocado, onion, and cheese), or our favorite, BLTCCB (bacon, lettuce, tomato, and cream cheese on a bagel).

Flat Bread: Use any of your favorite ingredients to create your own personal breakfast sandwich.

Most grocery stores dedicate a full aisle to about two hundred varieties of cereal. It is estimated that consumers spend nearly eight billion dollars on this popular convenience every year.

Breakfast FYI: According to Patti Worsley, who was born in Canada, there is no such thing as Canadian bacon, and it was never served for breakfast. A similar rumor is circulating in Belgium, says Belgian Vera Lauerhaas—there is no such thing as a Belgian waffle. There is a Brussels waffle, a light and fluffy 7 x 7–inch square served for dessert with fruit or ice cream. There also is a Luik waffle with sugar on the inside, but no Belgian breakfast waffle.

Noontime Whistle

Create your own culinary delights—something out of the ordinary. Mix colors, add layers, and top one side of the bread with a hot deli mustard and the other with a garlic mayonnaise. Use a bread that you have never tried before, a condiment from a foreign country, and add not one—but two!—vegetables to your creation.

Create beauty and your stomach will not be disappointed. Pack these masterpieces in school lunches, for picnics, or to take to the office and enjoy each bite outside for a twenty-five–minute break at noon. According to a recent article in *Vegetarian Times*, it takes twenty minutes for your stomach to notify your brain that it

Food eaten at a table is better for you than food eaten hunched over a desk, a counter, or driving in a car. And I believe that, wherever you do it, hurried eating has ruined more digestive systems than *foie gras*.

—Peter Mayle (b. 1939)

is satisfied. Follow the lead of our French sisters, who eat a leisurely and usually gourmet lunch. Slow your life for lunch.

For Crunchy Sandwiches:
- sesame seeds
- fennel seeds
- walnuts
- sliced almonds
- caraway seeds
- black peppercorns
- crispy bacon
- Macintosh apple slices
- pickles
- chopped celery

Essie Kenttala of Finland says she always eats her sandwiches open face. "We don't cover them like you do in the United States, but anything can be added, like cold smoked reindeer, ham, turkey, or other deli cuts with butter, cheese, tomatoes, cucumbers, pickles, or maybe a boiled egg."

Confetti Quesadillas: **Instead of creating a plain cheese quesadilla, give your lunch mates not only a serving of their daily required calcium, but also one or two of their vegetables. Add shredded cheese to a flour tortilla with corn, black beans, and chopped orange, green, and red bell peppers.**

After eating possibly more than two hundred sandwiches in a year, lunch between two slices of bread begins to lose its appeal to most. Other countries and cultures wrap this midday meal in a host of other options you might not have considered. Introduce your crew to a new way to enjoy lunch once again in an alternative to the traditional two white slices.

Circa 1762, John Montagu, the fourth earl of Sandwich, is credited for the creation of the sandwich. He supposedly did not want to leave the gaming table for lunch.

Our Daily Bread Options:

Foccacia

Rolls: potato, kaiser, onion, sesame, poppy seed, or plain

Bagel: any flavor

French baguette

Pita: sesame, garlic, or wheat

Tortillas: corn, flour, spinach, or tomato

Indian flatbreads: chapati, roti, or naan

> *Quick Lunch Fix*: Serve chicken or tuna salad as a dip with hearty crackers, carrots, and celery sticks.

In your lunch box today, use silverware and add a cloth napkin instead of paper. If lunching at home, set the table. These simple acts will make your entire day much brighter. Why reserve the beautiful things in your life just for holidays or certain days? Today is the day worth living for. Be there. Celebrate your life.

24–Hour Mom

In my research, I have now seen—or in this case, heard—it all. In a women's magazine, I stopped to read an ad for a refrigerator because I was in the market for one, but also because it made me laugh out loud. This refrigerator featured voice messaging "so now you can leave instructions for reheating dinners, shopping, or what the family can (and can't) eat when you're not able to be there."

> **Many hands make light work.**
> —*Amish saying*

Wow—is this what happens when mom cannot be there 24/7?

There has to be an easier and less expensive way to teach them to survive without us, like teaching our husbands and kids to cook, to be self-sufficient in this domain once reserved exclusively for women.

I say, "Share! Share in the shopping, the prepping, the stirring, and the cooking. Share in the learning and teaching of life skills with no gender biases."

Do away with the short-order cook position—it is usually the job Mom gets anyhow. Announce that from here on out the job has been eliminated in your kitchen, banished forever—unless someone else wants the job.

> There has always been a food processor in the kitchen, but once upon a time she was usually called the missus, or Mom.
> —Sue Berkman (b. 1936)

Make one meal a week a family affair with all participating. On another evening, encourage Dad to show off his culinary skills and treat the gang to a Western BBQ, but teach your kid(s), and maybe mom, too.

If the stove is still off limits for the younger set, let them be in charge of "Pizza Night," the night the kids get to "cook." Apart from the actual baking, be sure to relinquish the entire meal to them. Provide a premade crust, let them roll out freezer pizza dough from the grocery store, or use a loaf of French bread cut in half. Let them decorate the pizza with toppings and set the table (with paper goods, of course).

Remind them that clean up is part of dinner, too. Compliment the little chefs and allow them to relish the feeling of accomplishment from "doing it all by themselves." This new-found empowerment just might roll over to a surprise breakfast-in-bed on Saturday morning.

What's for Dinner?

Teach your family to cook, starting with the basics—sandwiches—but amaze Blondie and make Dagwood jealous. Build towering clubs, colorful open-face masterpieces, and hearty meals between two slices of bread. Adopt "Sandwich Night" as one of your regular, easy, and relaxing dinners of the week.

The Vietnamese wrap their food in just about everything from lettuce leaves to fresh rice paper. Give it a try for dinner tonight. In a wok, stir fry bite-sized chicken, black-bean sauce, garlic, and diced green onions together and serve in iceberg lettuce like a tortilla. It is a bit messy but quite tasty. On a hot summer night, this perfect mix of spicy and cool makes for great eating, especially outdoors.

See what you can create using other garden greens—such as endive, radicchio, bitter greens, and cabbage—to wrap a variety of fillings. All are excellent, low-calorie substitutes for bread.

Dear Santa: Ask Santa for a home-style *panini* grill to create a variety of hot grilled sandwiches for the winter months ahead.

Great Sandwich Condiments:

Rémoulade: Try this mayonnaise-like dressing made with mustard, also popularly flavored with chopped anchovies, capers, parsley, onions, garlic, and oil.

Salsa: Green chili, roasted garlic, peach, or mango—try them all.

Guacamole: Homemade, please: mash one avocado, and add salsa, garlic, and lemon.

Pesto: Take the shortcut and buy freshly prepared in your grocer's deli.

Mustard: Where to start? Whole grain, beer, Dijon, French, Tewkesbury, Bordeaux...

Balsamic vinegar and olive oil: Dress up your deli sandwich like a true submarine, hoagie, or hero sandwich.

Wasabi: Perfect if you prefer your sandwich with an extra bite.

> **Too few people understand a really good sandwich.**
> —*James Beard (1903–1985)*

Tabasco: The infamous hot sauce available in green and red varieties throughout the south, made from Tabasco peppers and by the same family since the 1870s.

Cranberry sauce: Not just for Thanksgiving anymore—great on turkey, and while you are at it, add a bit of stuffing, too.

No matter how you mash, slice, or cube the small, rough-to-the-touch Haas avocado, or the larger, bright green, smooth-skinned variety, both will deliver a punch of folic acid, iron, glutathione (an antioxidant that defends the body from free-radical attacks), magnesium, oleic acid, phosphorous, potassium, protein, and vitamin B6.

Sneak vegetables into every sandwich to eat your five servings or more of veggies daily.

Fresh Toppings:

- sliced mushrooms
- avocado slices
- marinated artichoke hearts
- fresh Italian parsley
- grilled peppers
- caramelized onions
- chopped onions
- poached asparagus
- capers
- grilled zucchini
- crushed garlic
- fresh thyme
- fresh rosemary

- fresh basil
- fresh dill
- dill or sweet relish
- shaved carrots
- sliced English or Japanese cucumber
- chives
- bamboo shoots
- sliced water chestnuts
- tomatoes
- olives: *Ligurian, Gaeta, Cerignola, Nicoise, Nyons, Picholine, Manzanilla, Arbequinas, Kalamata, Amphissa, Thasos, Nafplion, Elitses, or Sahli*

Kitchen Props for the Culinarily Challenged:

Vegetable Steamer (stainless steel or bamboo): Vegetables taste much better when steamed. Test often with a fork. Do not overcook. Drizzle lemon instead of butter or eat naked (the veggies, not you).

Circa 1830, ketchup became America's number-one condiment.

Clay Pot: This ancient invention is wonderful for busy people and does not stink up the kitchen when you bake fish. It does not hold the previous flavors of other meals, either.

Crock-Pot: Here is your answer to hired help. Prep the night before or in the morning and let this "cook" do the cooking all day long. Check out cookbooks from the library for 1,001 ideas.

Wok: Stir up dinner in half the time. Kids can even make stir-fried rice for dinner if you show them once. Add lots of vegetables and pork, chicken, or shrimp to make it heartier.

Rice Cooker: This is "no fail" rice cooking—honest. Try other rice types besides white— brown, basmati, jasmine, arborio—for a more nutritious and interesting meal.

Bread Machine: Dump in a boxed recipe, add the necessary (but easy) ingredients according to instructions, and enjoy fresh bread for breakfast or dinner. Most machines come with timers so you can bake while you are asleep or away from home.

Mortar and Pestle: Crush walnuts, pistachios, or pine or macadamia nuts or release the flavor of fennel seeds, garlic, and fresh herbs with this old-fashioned kitchen tool. Once positioned on your countertop, you might look for new herbs to try and even entertain offers from smaller hands to help you.

Tea Kettle: A must for the top of all stoves for a cup of tea or instant Chinese noodles, soup, hot cocoa, apple cider, Cream of Wheat, or oatmeal.

Keep It Simple

For Wednesday night's simple dinner, announce that it is "Hearty Soup Night." Pick up a can or two of the family's favorite soups. In a vegetable-based soup, toss in extra carrots, frozen peas, corn, spinach, or okra to make it your own creation. Garnish tomato soup with cilantro or shredded cheddar cheese. Add extra basil, oregano, or croutons to minestrone. Crumble bacon atop a bowl of New England clam chowder. Serve garlic bread, breadsticks, flatbread, or crackers, too. Don't forget the candles and dessert.

By the end of the winter, you may have created a dozen new ways to spice up the good old standbys and created the confidence in a younger member of the household to take

> **I no longer prepare food or drink with more than one ingredient.**
> —*Cyra McFadden (b. 1937)*

over on Wednesday nights.

On Friday nights, decide to "go out to dinner." Set the table with a red-and-white checkered tablecloth, make a beautiful garden salad, add a basket of crunchy garlic bread for the night's centerpiece, and put on opera music such as: *The Most Famous Opera Arias* by Encore or *Movies Go to the Opera Vol. II* from Angel Records.

For this "Pasta Night" served at home, you must offer a choice of "gravies" as any good Italian restaurant would. Serve a choice of Alfredo sauce, roasted garlic and onion marinara, or sun-dried tomato sauce (yes, all from a jar, but read the label—the shorter the ingredient list, the better) or simply dress the noodles with freshly grated Parmesan and toss with a little extra virgin olive oil and crushed black pepper.

Tonight, you and your dining guests will be instantly transported to a tiny *ristorante* in the south of Italy without getting on an airplane.

The Art of Interpretive Cooking

One reason why many people (myself included), abhor cooking, baking, and other culinary acrobatics is due to the rules and regulations of the kitchen bibles—the cookbooks. Even the recipes touted as "easy" and "simple" aren't. Unless you have an extra

> *Rule of Herb*: One tablespoon of chopped fresh herbs is equivalent to one teaspoon of dried herbs.

three hours in the day or a backup crew of line chefs standing ready, plus a pantry equivalent to a five-star restaurant's, most of us default to prepackaged or fast food.

The night is just too short to tackle the gastronomic equivalent of the SAT in the kitchen.

My advice is to keep it simple, truly simple, whether it is another family dinner or a celebration for a graduate. I think we need a truly elementary cookbook, filled with full-page, beautiful photos of what the dish could look like, and a list of the ingredients (without any measurements) to relax the restrictions around daily cooking. Isn't this what our foremothers used to do? They verbally shared recipes, saying, "With a bit of this and a tad of that..." and they didn't even have a photo for reference...

With these lower expectations, creativity (and novices) will be invited back into the kitchen. Substitutions and short cuts allowed without apologies. Add a little color, a new spice, something sweet and sour on the menu, and candles. Candles will make any dish taste wonderful, even if your creation is simply macaroni and cheese.

Healthy Options:

· Make fruit kebabs for tonight's dessert.
· Try salsa instead of dressing.
· For a veggie dip, sample hummus: roasted garlic, roasted red pepper, spicy pepper, or eggplant.
· Buy local fruit, vegetables, eggs, chicken, and meats to serve.
· Spike your pitcher of water with lime pinwheels or a few juicy chunks of watermelon.
· Freeze blueberries, raspberries, or slices of strawberries in ice cubes and add vitamin C to your glass of water.
· Offer vegetable or fruit juices, or iced or hot herbal teas as alternative beverage choices.

> I have always believed that opera is a planet where the muses work together, join hands and celebrate all the arts.
> —*Franco Zeffirelli (b. 1923)*

> I cooked once in 1978 and decided it was a bad idea.
> —*M(ary) G(race) Lord (b. 1955)*

> I feel a recipe is only a theme, which an intelligent cook can play each time with a variation.
> —*Madame Benoit (1904–1987)*

In the fourth century BC, Athenian cooks were oftentimes slaves, but they were given the power to rule over the other slaves in the household. A special law in Rome allowed the cook who invented a new recipe to sell it to the public. Many Greek cooks became famous due to their daily toil in the kitchen.

Have you thought about selling your culinary talents? Host a party to test the recipes—your friends and family will surely oblige. You are more qualified to venture into this realm than you may think. Haven't you sampled foods for decades?

Be curious, be adventurous, and only invite those to the dinner or party table who will appreciate your interpretation of culinary creativity. This is the way that my sister cooks, and it is always wonderful. Remember, any reason for a bash—and a new recipe (yours) definitely calls for one.

Teresa Lust, author of *Pass the Polenta* says, "Baking is a science, but cooking—well cooking is art—simply use the recipe as a guideline, add a bit of patience and a couple of stirs with a wooden spoon and you have greatness in a dish."

This week, test different approaches to cooking with reckless abandon. With ethnic food being the new *haute* cuisine, create Latin dishes with Douglas Rodriguez as your personal guide. Chinese-American chef Patricia Yeo will direct

> **Poultry is for the cook what canvas is for the painter.**
> —*Jean Anthelme Brillat-Savarin (1775–1826)*

New Twist on Oils: Experiment with different cooking oils to bring a new and perhaps lighter taste to your table:

- Flip pancakes or waffles with sweet almond or walnut oil.
- Bake corn muffins with sunflower or corn oil.
- Grease baking pans with grapeseed or canola oil (known as rapeseed outside the U.S.).
- Stir fry with safflower, sesame, or peanut oil.
- Sauté any dish made with garlic or onions in olive oil.

you around the Oriental kitchen in any of her cookbooks. Follow Charles Phan's culinary words of advice and whip up a Vietnamese dish tonight. Take a trip to the warm Caribbean with Jamaican-born Cheryl Smith, and pepper your meal with spices new to your palate.

Be willing to be surprised and surprise those who turn up for tonight's party with a culinary theme from another country.

Just Desserts

In 1991, I bought *Eat Dessert First* by Steve Wilson. While I have made a point of offering my family healthy alternatives to prepackaged and fast foods, dessert occasionally eaten first is a great way to celebrate life. Try any of these suggestions, but have a heavy hand on the fruit over the other ingredients:

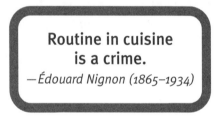

> **Cookery is not chemistry. It is an art. It requires instinct and taste rather than exact measurements.**
> —*Marcel Boulestin aka John Francis Toye (1883–1964)*

> **Routine in cuisine is a crime.**
> —*Édouard Nignon (1865–1934)*

Fondue Fruit: Try summer and exotic fruit: cherries, peaches, apricots, apples, bananas, figs, pineapple, papaya, mangoes, and star fruit. Hold fruit in a bowl of cold water to keep fresh and to keep from browning. Squeeze lime juice on bananas. Pull out the fondue pot and the caramels or chocolate bars and have dipped fruit for dessert.

Berries-and-Cream Sundaes: Use any summertime berries: strawberries, blueberries, blackberries, Marionberries, or raspberries with any cream—whipped or ice cream. Note the emphasis is on the berries, not the cream.

Fresh Fruit Sorbet: Homemade or store bought, just buy the kind made only with fresh fruit.

Individual Tart Shells: Fill store-bought pastry shells with lemon curd or lemon pudding. On top, arrange a dozen (or more) fresh berries.

Pound Cake: Again, let the baker (or grocery store) do the baking and serve a slice of pound cake with sliced strawberries and a fresh sprig of mint. Lightly sprinkle your fresh creation with powdered sugar.

Playing with Food

One winter night my family and I decided to have fondue for dinner. We now call this special meal together "fun food" because we get to eat with our hands. It all started with good intentions of using the fondue forks; then we tried chopsticks, which still did not do the job. Knives and spoons were used to salvage the lost pieces of bread, baby carrots, sugar-snap peas, yellow bell peppers, asparagus spears, and chicken in the thick, gooey, bubbling cheese. We finally resorted to pulling and picking with our fingers. Miss Manners would have been offended, but eating our dinner this way made the food taste great. We were part of the meal and the meal was part of us. Our "fun-food fondue" is now a regular request. (Not too often—we don't want the novelty to wear off!)

Now we are always looking for new ingredients to dunk, swirl, and save from the strong gridlock grip of the melted cheese. From soft cheeses such as Chevre or goat's milk cheese or firm options like Appenzeller, Gruyère, and Emmenthaler (which need to be cooked with wine or lemon juice), to easier first-time fondue choices of cheddar, fontina, Edam, mozzarella, and Beaufort, the choices are many. Try out a fondue cookbook and discover how simple this meal can truly be. After mastering cheese fondue, move on to cooking bite-sized pieces of meat and fish tabletop using oils such as corn, vegetable, soya, or sunflower. Of course, you must then try your hand at chocolate and berry puree fondues.

Emergency Rescue

Secrets told through the kitchen back doors of professional chefs, off the record by the authors of the best cookbooks, and in the well-stocked

> **Dining is and always was a great artistic opportunity.**
> —*Frank Lloyd Wright (1869–1959)*

pantries of amateur cooks reveal all kinds of culinary short cuts. So, if these masters can, you should, too. Borrow from their experience and make the meal event much easier.

This emergency stock of foods in your pantry will allow a simple dinner to be made easily and without stress:

Canned tomatoes: Use pureed tomatoes as a soup base, choose basil-flavored or whole canned tomatoes to make a sauce, or select diced to make Spanish rice.

Beans: Collect every color and flavor: black beans, white or red kidney, Navy, or refried. (Be sure to rinse and drain canned whole beans before using.)

Round Breads: Fill pitas or top a flour or corn tortilla with cheese, lettuce, chopped chicken, pork, shrimp, beef, or steamed vegetables.

Pasta: Keep a supply of all shapes and sizes on hand. Toss with olive oil, Greek olives, and fresh Parmesan. Make a vegetable pasta salad or a cold tuna and pasta salad.

Rice: Try wild, white, or brown, or aromatic rice such as basmati, jasmine, or Della, and arborio, typically used in risotto. Add frozen peas, corn, scrambled eggs, and fish, and serve piping hot as a wonderful, one-dish meal.

Ancient Grains: Slow cooking, but well worth the time for the flavor and nutrition: barley, amaranth, Kamut, rye, faro, millet, spelt, or quinoa.

Fonduta is the Italian version of fondue made with a mixture of cheeses: fontina, provolone, dolcelatte, or Gorgonzola.

Veggie chili made from canned beans and tomatoes is a quick fix for dinner. Toss in some diced onions, serve with a thick slice of bread, and keep it a secret.

Parties around the Table

Amidst all of the noise and interruptions in our world—cell phones (now everyone in the entire family may have one), pagers, the daily deluge of snail mail and email, and the usual list of 101 things to do—it is no wonder the average American is exhausted at the end of most days.

Lose the hurry at dinnertime. Lose the routine. Get out of the rut. To get your family back around the table together and back to balanced and healthy eating, employ any of these unique twists on the same old dinners to make any meal a party at home:

The Other Rice: Couscous, the popular mainstay of North African cuisine, consists of small grains, of which semolina is the main ingredient. Since it resembles rice, couscous is oftentimes called its cousin.

Dinner Quick Fix:
Shrimp and Mango Salad
    1 bag of washed greens
    1 mango
    1½ cups peeled, cooked shrimp
    1 jar of tricolored peppers
    1 red onion
    1 avocado
Slice and combine the ingredients, and toss with a bit of balsamic vinegar and olive oil. This is one great salad that covers all the bases: vegetables, protein, color, and taste.

Impromptu Indoor Picnics: On a blustery winter night, unpack the picnic basket right in the middle of the living room floor. Break open a package of decorative paper napkins, matching paper plates, and a tablecloth. Today *is* that special day—celebrate your life now with those you love. Select your picnic music to bring back memories of summer—anything by the Beach Boys, or try Jorma Kaukonen's *Blue Country Heat,* or Leftover Salmon's *O Cracker Where Art Thou?* Serve light cuisine and sit down for a mini-vacation from the "humdrum" of every-night dinners.

"To Go" Chinese Food Dinners: Ask the last one coming home tonight to pick up the Chinese food. While you are waiting, transform your living room into an exotic restaurant with a low table, comfy pillows, chopsticks, fortune cookies, and a pot of oolong tea. (No shoes.)

Movie-themed Dinner: I am not a big advocate of watching television while eating, especially with the ceaseless advertising of nonnutritional snacks and drinks parading every ten minutes, but a good movie is another story and a great excuse to celebrate another meal.

Since these celebratory movies emphasize the seduction of food and the power of good company to draw people together, consider any of these recommendations and perhaps be inspired to design a corresponding menu for tonight's spontaneous party with good friends:

- *Babette's Feast*
- *Big Night*
- *Four Weddings & A Funeral*
- *Fried Green Tomatoes*
- *Like Water for Chocolate*
- *Monsoon Wedding*
- *My Big Fat Greek Wedding*
- *Tortilla Soup*

> ## Serve the dinner backwards, do anything—but for goodness sake, do something weird.
> —Elsa Maxwell (1883–1963)

Silent Meals: During these "silent dinners," talking is allowed while prepping, but once the meal is served, "Shhhh"—for the entire main course. Put a caddy on the table to catch the quarters of those who cannot refrain from talking. At dessert, let the conversation begin. Use the money collected by the end of the year and head out for a rowdy night at the local diner or burger joint.

Whisper Dinners: If your supper club cannot eat without talking, then try the "whisper meal" option. With the volume of the day usually on loud, this whisper dinner once in a while will be a welcome escape from the din of the world. Sit back and watch the soothing effect that this meal has over the entire family and you.

Musical Meals: Tonight, design your menu around the music. Grilling a rack of ribs tonight? Turn up the country music. Let the good music emit a good energy into the fading hours of the day.

Dress-Up Meals: Feel a need to use the fancy dishes more than once a year? Why save your party dresses and tuxedo for a special occasion? Light the taper candles, dress the table in fine linens, bring out the forgotten china, and make Saturday night at home the reason for this celebration. Have a little one in the house make place markers for your dinner guests—your family. Be creative and let them use their imagination and whatever art supplies are in the house. Ask your partner to pick up a box of Andes mints to serve at the conclusion of this truly wonderful meal. Put on classical music as a guaranteed mood enhancer, and dine elegantly tonight no matter what the menu is.

Pajama Meals: On other nights, forget the pomp and circumstance and the strict rule of no pajamas at the table. Reserve tonight as the night to serve breakfast for dinner: cereal, hot or cold, or perhaps something a bit more substantial—eggs, sausage, ham, potatoes, pancakes, waffles, muffins, or bread loaded with walnuts, cranberries, blueberries, or whatever is the family favorite.

Insist on baths first—including a luxurious one for mom—and then serve breakfast for the second time today. At this comfy and relaxed gathering, fuzzy slippers and bathrobes are also permitted.

Table for One: Dine *al fresco* tonight, complete with white-clothed table illuminated with a half dozen taper candles and a single rosebud crowning your place setting. In this elegant setting, serve yourself a simple, yet hearty meal of soup and country bread.

Musical Entrees:
Hawaiian: Taj Mahal and The Hula Blues, *Hanapepe Dream*
South Hemisphere: *An Afro-Portuguese Odyssey*
Cajun: Buckwheat Zydeco and company, *Tomorrow's Zydeco*

Add any concerto by Vivaldi, an overture by Bach, symphony by Beethoven, or piano concerto by Mozart, and your company will enjoy their dinner doubly tonight.

One does not age at the table.
—*Grimod de la Reynière (1758–1838)*

chapter 3

merry
DAYS

*twelve heartwarming invitations

Life itself is the proper binge.
—*Julia Child (b. 1912)*

The twelve invitations that follow are reminders that no month should pass without reflection on how lucky we are to be alive. In the survey for this book, most women only reported celebrating four to six times a year—out of 365 opportunities!

This is your guide to creating a fun outing, hosting a surprise party, or making a special moment for someone who may need it the most—you. These celebratory ideas can also be shared with family and friends. All of the party themes and recipes are simple to implement and encourage activities to try as well.

Promise you will indulge at least once every thirty days. It is important to honor your days—no matter how small the party or occasion. From January to December, use any of these excuses to celebrate, or make up your own. There are no rules, no proper etiquette; the only required ingredients are love and attention.

January
"Me Time"

After the holidays, the last thing you probably want to do is host a party. Most likely, a moment of solitude sounds like a good idea right now—so do it. On your calendar, circle a January date and invite yourself to a quiet place and time. From the approximately 720 hours in every month, you can and should reserve at least two or three just for you.

Within your home, choose a tranquil place that allows you to think and be still, or choose to go out into nature and be awakened by winter's freshness.

Enter a world new to you: tour a museum exhibit or attend a gallery opening. Pack a picnic lunch with your favorite food and beverage—or treat yourself to lunch or dinner out. No fast-food stops; instead choose a funky diner, a teahouse, or an elegant restaurant—whatever piques your curiosity at the moment.

> Discovery consists not in seeking new landscapes but in having new eyes.
> —*Marcel Proust (1871–1922)*

The Red Balloon Tradition: My good friend, Johnnie Lucero, has started an annual tradition in honor of her life. At the start of each year, she purchases a red helium balloon (not Mylar) and lets it go. As she watches the balloon climb higher into the sky, she affirms her intentions to allow her creative spirit to soar higher in the coming year.

Take along a sketchpad and pencils, your journal for creative ideas or mental ramblings about life as you see it, or a camera to capture the beauty of the world.

Go somewhere, go anywhere, and go alone, too, so you can hear your own thoughts without any distractions. During this time, leave the cell phone (and pager) turned off—no one else is invited. In these few stolen hours, become your own best friend. Listen to your inner voice, your thoughts, and find out who you are and what you truly enjoy. This month, seek silence and solitude. It is exactly what your mind, body, and spirits need at the start of a New Year.

February
Chocolate Fondue Party

February is all about romance and couples, but what about the other people in our lives who also matter? I propose that you save the fourteenth for your significant other and another date later in the month for your movie-buff friends.

Rent the movie *Chocolat*, and instruct those invited to bring a fondue pot and their favorite dipping food: biscotti, small cubes of firm-textured cakes, cookies, or fruit. You provide the different hot sauces for dipping, such as dark or milk chocolate, white chocolate, raspberry chocolate, espresso chocolate, or pear-cinnamon caramel.

This ceremonial ritual is perfect for a few good friends and might become a new monthly tradition.

Chocolate, introduced to Spain by Hermán Cortéz, came along in the form of hot chocolate. Its fame as an aphrodisiac spread throughout Europe and forced women who fancied the drink to imbibe in secret.

Chocolate, so popular in Europe and the United States, has yet to catch on in Asia or Africa.

March
Muse Gatherings

This party idea is ideal for poets, novelists, essayists, screenplay writers, playwrights, artists, musicians, and singers—anyone who wants a safe forum in which to release their creative talent into the world. Early in the month, send the invitations to encourage like minds to unite where confidence can grow and new voices can be found and heard.

On opening night, create a Bohemian parlor with thick, padded floor pillows and comfy blankets. Illuminate the room with a few scented candles, such as those infused with the essential oil of rosemary, pine, or jasmine to promote courage and mental clarity. However, make sure the articulate artist has ample light.

In ancient Greece and Rome, poets, athletes, and victorious soldiers wore crowns of honor made from laurel, which also is known today as the common herb, bay leaves.

Spring Equinox: Each year, when the sun crosses the equator about March 21, it makes the night and day of equal length all over the world. Perhaps the change in light on this date is as good a reason as any for creative spirits to convene.

Try this icebreaker to interject a bit of humor and relax nervous jitters before the evening begins: greet each guest at the door and request they wear an honorary crown of laurel.

Without judgment or competition, give each guest an opportunity to present their work in a respectful silence and with a floor open for positive thoughts, comments, or suggestions. At the close of the evening, make a pact to meet again, ensuring your guests finish a work for the next creative gathering.

April
Good Karma

The first day of April, with its spontaneous jokes and tricks, usually lands someone as the butt of a joke. This year, decide to put a different spin on the punch line and make these surprises a good thing in someone's life.

Since the underlying message of this book is to remind all of us to celebrate our lives—each and every day—we need to tell those who surround us, those who make up our lives, how much we care. Acknowledge and be grateful for all that you have: your family, your friends, and the circle of people in your town or city, your schools, and your work. This recognition of others who make our lives a tad easier will continue to spread goodwill.

A spoken "thank you," a smile of gratitude, a written thank-you note, or a thank-you gift—any means will express your appreciation for this particular person. Use your imagination, not your credit card, to make a difference in someone else's life today, and then stand back and be amazed how much more fulfilled you and your life will become.

For no reason at all, send surprise mail to a friend, family member, or business associate—someone you know who works too hard. It could be a funny greeting card, a fortune cookie, or a postcard from your hometown.

Instead of driving and shopping for a greeting card, use the time and energy to make your own instead. Keep a stash of favorite greeting cards sent by others, cut the front off and recycle it into a postcard. Buy fancy-scented stationery or make your own personal sheets with the help of clip art and the computer. Whatever works—and most times, anything from the heart will.

> **The most radiant woman in the room is the one full of life experience.**
> —*Sharon Stone (b.1958)*

My dad is the king of Post-it note letters. He writes to me on these tiny pieces of paper attached to articles clipped from newspapers and magazines. His letters are several pages long—full of only essential words—but regardless, I have good news mail, and from my father no less.

> **Gratitude is the heart's memory.**
> —*French proverb*

Whenever I miss my family members who are scattered across the country, I start a postcard campaign. I send postcards of skiing, the rodeo, and the Yampa River rippling in early June due to the high mountain snow melt—snapshots from my life, taken by a professional photographer. The unsuspecting relative receives about ten to twelve of these "invitations" to come visit anytime. My sister, brother, dad, or cousin usually arrives in eight months or less. This subtle hint works well with long-lost friends, too.

Make sure your circle of friends and family receive their share of good news via "snail" mail rather than just email. There is something special about receiving a handwritten note from someone who cares about you.

Send some happy mail today to those who matter in your life, no matter what day it is. You will brighten their day for sure.

Surprise someone who deserves the recognition with an unexpected gift. Maybe this person is a teacher from elementary-school days or college who inspired you to do your very best. (You can still hear her words.) Send her a gift, small or not, handmade or store purchased. Do it now—in spite of the many years that have passed. It will mean the world to her.

The author of *Making a Literary Life: Advice for Writers and Other Dreamers*, Carolyn See, tells her students to write thank-you notes to authors whose work they admire or to send them a bouquet of balloons.

"Why?" they ask. "What is in it for me?" "Why would this person I don't know even care what I think?" These are the common rebuttals that Ms. See receives at the start of her class, but by the end, some authors have written back to the students to say, "Thank you."

What a difference two words can make in everyone's world.

May
Kaffeeklatsch Parties

In the early 1600s, the word *coffee* first appeared in the English language. It is thought to be a derivative of the Turkish word, *kahveh*, which means, "a wine tonic that restores the appetite," perhaps the perfect excuse—prior to dinner—to celebrate each day.

Other connoisseurs say coffee is called coffee because these trees have grown wild since ancient times in the province of Kaffa in Ethiopia.

According to ancient legend, a Moslem religious man noticed that the goats in Yemen appeared livelier than others when they feasted on the berries of a prominent growing plant of the area. To test the theory that they might have the same effect on humans, he roasted the beans, ground them, and made an infusion. The result? Coffee as we know it today.

Do you crave the company of a few witty and wise women? Reintroduce the German concept of afternoon coffee. (Perhaps the first order of business among friends is to sort out where, indeed, the word *coffee* comes from—and how was it ever nicknamed "a cup of Joe" anyhow?) Adjust the idea of having good coffee and good conversation to fit in your world. What about Saturday mornings with the next-door neighbors twice a month? Make invitations zipped off the computer, or handwritten notes, and drop them at your friends' front doors. An email invitation or telephone call will work just as well.

Take a midmorning break at work with business associates at a local coffee shop. Talk business if you must, but go for a walk.

If the weekends are busy with the kids' sports, pack a thermos to take along to the soccer game and share with the other mothers. Bring iced coffee if the day's temperature warrants something cold—and don't forget the picnic blanket.

But when you do invite friends to your house for a cup of coffee, make it a *special* cup of java. Try any of these ideas to explore the faraway corners of the world that have perfected the perfect cup.

Between 1880 and 1889, the word *kaffeeklatsch* appeared in German and means "coffee and noise" (e.g., conversation).

We are here to awaken from the illusion of our separateness.
—*Thich Nhat Hanh (b. 1926)*

The Isle of Patmos: To create the illusion of the Greek Isles, layer the senses of sight and sound on your patio. Decorate an outdoor table with a crisp, white tablecloth and fresh flowers, play *Nana Mouskouri: At Her Very Best,* and capture the feeling of sitting under cerulean skies in the Aegean islands. Entice your friends to linger with a little steaming cup of thick Greek coffee, served with a delicious square of baklava.

Café Italiano: For a new twist on your coffee time, take your group to Italy. Bake or buy a couple of different types of biscotti and serve with a tiny cup of espresso. Purchase whole-bean coffee labeled Italian or espresso to ensure a smooth, rich cup. Add a bit of opera, either *Puccini and Pasta* or Andrea Bocelli's *Romanza* to further wake up the mind and body. Your friends will not be saying "*Ciao!*" anytime soon.

Jamaican Afternoons: Let the air be filled with a song by Bob Marley and the aroma of Blue Mountain coffee, straight from the island of Jamaica itself. Splash your gathering area with bright colors—canary yellow, chartreuse, and passion-fruit purple—to brighten the day, as a fan gently stirs the warm air. Serve a platter of sliced and cubed tropical fruit sprinkled with coconut shavings.

Plantains are a popular "chip" served almost anytime of the day in Jamaica. With a steaming cup of coffee and a tasty treat, you might succeed in creating the fantasy that all of you are truly away on a Caribbean holiday. Your friends may enjoy sitting in paradise so much that it will be easy to get them to return, and often.

Once a month (or sooner), let a new hostess decide which country to visit and serve the appropriate coffee. The fun challenge will be to create the atmosphere of another place where time moves according to your whims, not your watch.

Cultural Differences: Mormons do not drink anything that is stimulating such as alcohol or coffee, but Muslims, who also abhor alcohol, consider their daily cup of coffee *de rigueur*.

Spicy Conversations

In Arabic countries, cardamom is added to coffee because it is believed that the spice stimulates conversation and good feelings among friends.

Cardamom is also esteemed in the Bedouin culture. According to a long-standing tradition, whenever guests arrive and before they are served cardamom coffee, a plump, blemish-free pod is displayed, implying respect for the guests.

In Scandinavian countries, this sweet yet peppery spice is added to cakes, pastries, and breads. Could this spice alone be the excuse to bake something new for Sunday brunch and offer a new cup of flavored coffee to friends and family?

Some countries for the perfect bean theme:

- Arabia
- Brazil
- Colombia
- Ethiopia
- Guatemala
- Hawaii
- Indonesia
- Kenya
- Sulawesi
- Sumatra
- Yemen

Root Controller by Misty in Roots is an excellent comilation of Rasta ideology and spirit told through talented bass, horn, and keyboard artists.

June
Journaling Sessions

Why keep a journal? A personal journal allows frustrations to dissipate as well as happy memories to be preserved, which might otherwise be forgotten in the years to come. The act of writing your thoughts, ideas, opinions, and dreams down on paper possesses power and magic. By allowing your hand to write what your mind is thinking and your body is feeling, you can fully express yourself. This quiet time spent alone will expand your creative ideas and thoughts, improve relationships, allow for emotional and spiritual growth, and result in a greater appreciation of life.

For this occasion—yes, it is a party—treat yourself to a new pen and beautiful journal. Do not edit. Do not fix spelling mistakes or critique your handwriting—anything is permitted. There is no judgment here on these pages; it is simply your place to be right all the time. This is your time, your spot in the universe, where your words are perfect and unconditionally accepted. You are understood.

Enhance your journaling experience with aromatherapy—a wonderful way to make an ordinary day special, even just for an hour. The essential oils of neroli, ylang-ylang, or juniper will do wonders for your spirit, especially on low energy days. Add a few drops to an unscented candle, and carefully light it before you begin to write. Breathe in its soothing aroma.

You can also add several drops to a steaming bowl of hot water. Stir gently to release the delicate yet powerful essence. Now you are ready.

Capture Your Dreams

It never fails. Whenever I get into the bathtub (my other peaceful sanctuary besides my nap sanctuary), in about seven minutes the ideas start to flow. Then I have the choice of

> **Do we not live in dreams?**
> —Alfred Lord Tennyson (1809–1892)

climbing out of the warm water and dripping across the bathroom and bedroom to my office for paper and pen, or just trying to remember them all. The other day I told my good friend about my dilemma and she said, "Why don't you keep a journal by the tub?"

It is always easier to see the solution for someone else's problem. (Thanks, Elizabeth!) Let your journal (or your friends) help you find the answers.

Journaling Together

Plan journaling sessions among an intimate group of friends to guarantee that you will write in your journal regularly. As any good party planner knows, the question of where to host the event always plays heavily into the success of the gathering. For these types of soul-baring adventures, I suggest your group take a hike. You decide whether it is best to go at first daybreak or follow the setting sun (bring flashlights).

Walk for a while and then make camp in a park, open grove, orchard, or forest. You may suggest a theme for your group to write about—tomatoes, hope, the color blue—or encourage them to write a letter never to be mailed. Separate and write for twenty or thirty minutes. Be respectful of this time. Remain silent or speak in low whispers so as not to disturb those who are finishing.

The option of sharing your writings is up to each individual, with no questions asked or opinions aired.

Next month, return to the same spot (together or not), but do make a deal with yourself to write again. You need to hear what your mind, body, and spirit are telling you. Open your journal regularly, and be ready with a pen to capture whatever you dream.

July
Salad Luncheon Party

In writing this third book in the *Permission* book series, I once again sent surveys to women all over the country, this time to discover what they did to celebrate. Did they consider themselves "party goddesses" or would they rather have root canals? Was a big ordeal required to call it a party, or could a few friends over for a salad lunch be called a celebration?

I say "yes" to all. Any moment spent in recognition of great food and great friends (you included) is a party in my book.

A fellow ambassador at the Steamboat ski resort, Louise Poppen, told me about her frequent salad parties. She calls her good friends and asks each of them to bring over an ingredient, washed, chopped, or sliced and ready to be added to the big salad bowls. Together, they create a beautiful work of art to be shared over good conversation.

Happy Salads: Consider any of the following ingredients not only for their bright, happy colors, but also for their healthful properties:

Carrots: Sliced, diced, or shredded, carrots are not only good for your eyes, but for the rest of your body, too. Medical studies have shown carrot juice to ease menopausal symptoms and contribute to the prevention of cancer, especially breast cancer.

Radishes: Here in the States, the cherry-sized red radishes are the most popular; however, the next time you roam a farmer's market, search for other varieties: black, white, or the long-rooted option. This vegetable, rich in phosphorous, potassium, selenium (a nutrient necessary for prevention of heart disease and cancer), and vitamin C is a good addition to your basket.

Tomatoes: Include any of these superb, garden-fresh pickings in your next sandwich, salad, chutney, or salsa: cherry tomato, heirloom, green tomatoes, Beefsteak, Roma, or yellow pear, and you will not be disappointed. Known for their cancer-fighting properties (especially prostate) with the compound lycopene (a carotene) tomatoes are a daily must for you and any men in your life.

Borrow Louise's idea—I am sure that she won't mind. If you do not get around to hosting your salad luncheon until the ground freezes over, tweak the concept a bit and toss all the ingredients into a big pot of simmering chicken broth or a tomato base. On the coldest of nights, celebrate "Soup Night" to warm up with good food and good friends.

> **A simple salad can be pure heaven.**
> —*Emeril Lagasse (b. 1960)*

Lastly, you can twist this collective-sharing idea and invite a few families for a backyard "Grill Off." Each crew is to bring something to grill—basted or marinated in the chef's prized BBQ sauce. Share everything, let the taste testing begin, and vote for your favorite.

August
Beach Parties

Some summers just fly by without the opportunity to pack it up and head to the shore. Between the kids' sports and work at the office and around the house, lazy time spent on the beach seems to be a distant memory. You can change this.

This weekend, invite your friends to a beach party at your house. Give it a Hawaiian theme and grace the table with all types of tidbits that are good for you: dried papaya slices, fresh pineapple chunks, and mango shakes served in coconut shells sipped through a curly straw. Blow up beach balls and inflatable palm trees, keep iced drinks in personal sand buckets, offer a collection of suntanning lotions, big floppy hats, beach towels, the sound of the surf (compliments of a hidden sound machine), and hopefully, a sunny afternoon. Who says you have to be on a tropical island to enjoy its benefits?

If the day is a scorcher, take a break from the sun and create your own signature smoothies. Ask each beach guest to bring one of these healthy additives:

Carob: Ground from the pods of the Mediterranean evergreen tree, carob is a good substitute for those sensitive to the caffeine found in chocolate. It is also low in fat and a good source of calcium.

Honey: Bees visit all types of flowers and grains to bring a unique flavor to your jar of sweetness. In addition to orange blossom, clover, and alfalfa honey, give buckwheat—the dark and robust cousin—a taste, or safflower, sage, heather, or even thyme. It is best to avoid those honeys from commercially raised bees fed sugar water or corn syrup. Also keep an eye out for unheated, unfiltered, or unprocessed honey.

> *Half and Half Summer* wonderfully refreshi beverage, mix a pitcher of iced tea and lemonade together. Float a few lemon pinwheels on top of the ice cubes.

> The lighter the color of honey, the milder the flavor.

Bee Pollen: With amino acids, B-complex vitamins, carotenes, calcium, copper, iron, magnesium, manganese, polyunsaturated fatty acids, potassium, protein, and sodium, a little dash of bee pollen can also help with seasonal allergies if a local brand can be found. Look for this supplement in the refrigerated section of your health-food store.

Ginseng: Trying to kick or at least reduce your caffeine consumption? Ginseng just might do the trick. Available in three varieties: Siberian, American, and Panax, this herb is a natural energizer. In addition to helping fight colds and reduce stress, it protects the lungs, enhances the immune system, and normalizes blood pressure. Best to add ginseng in liquid form as an extract, which can be found at most natural-food stores.

Spirulina: High in protein and minerals, rich in iron, potassium, calcium, gamma-linolenic acid, vitamin B12, amino acids, chlorophyll, and phycocyanin (a pigment with anticancer properties), this popular microalgae protects the immune system, reduces cholesterol, and assists in mineral absorption. Spirulina, an excellent detoxifier that cleanses the body of pollutants and other toxins, is actually a single-celled algae found in fresh-water lakes and ponds.

Coconut: Coconut is rich in magnesium, a nutrient that a woman's body demands during pregnancy.

Dates: Deglet Noor, Khadrawy, Thoory, Halawi, or Medjool dates, loaded with calcium, magnesium, and phosphorus, are instrumental in building strong bones and teeth. Your fresh, sweet treats should be stored in the refrigerator, but can also be frozen and added to your smoothies at a later date. Great eaten naked (without any sugar or corn syrup added). Try to avoid those packaged with preservatives: potassium sorbate, sorbic acid, sodium benzoate, or sulfur dioxide.

Mangos: Eating a diet rich in the colors of orange, red, and dark green will help you to live a long, healthy life because of the carotenes these fruits and vegetables contain. Always peel your mangos; those arriving from foreign ports may still use carcinogenic sprays, which are illegal in the United States.

Apricots: Choose any kind of this golden-orange–colored fruit: Blenheim, Tilton, Early Montgamet, or Wenatchee. A good source of calcium, you will benefit from this sweet fruit rich in carotenes and flavonoids.

Pineapples: Choose from Pernambuco, Queen, or Red Spanish, or go with the most popular, Smooth Cayenne, and you are on your way to getting your daily dose of calcium, iron, iodine, magnesium, potassium, and bromelain, an enzyme that aids in the digestion of protein.

Papayas: Like mangos and many of the imported golden-orange or deep-yellow treats, papaya is rich in betacarotene, vitamin C, and the protein-digesting enzyme papain. Always remove the skin; in some countries, the fruit may still be sprayed with carcinogenic agents.

Bananas: Your source for chromium, iron, magnesium, potassium, and vitamin B6. Plus, any smoothie made with bananas will be even smoother.

Got Soy?

You don't have to forgo shakes and smoothies if you are lactose intolerant. Soy is your answer for more than one good reason. The most intriguing and interesting compounds of soy are its isoflavones—genistein, daidzein, and glycitein—which function similarly to human estrogen, exerting a balancing effect on hormonal levels.

Smoothie Hints:

- In the blender, add raw, unsalted cashews with other ingredients to make your smoothie creamy the way milk does.
- Brew a pot of chamomile, green, peach, or chai tea, or any of your favorite herbal infusions. When the tea cools, freeze it in ice cube trays and add to your shake recipe.
- Instead of sugar, try honey or pure maple syrup to sweeten your breakfast drink (a little goes a long way).
- Instead of plain tofu, try soft silken tofu. This soybean curd is sweeter with higher water content and has a custard-like texture. Rich in protein, it also contains lecithin to help lower blood pressure and promote the utilization of fat.

This healthy additive also provides anticarcinogenic and antiangiogenic properties, boosting your immune system and benefiting your heart. New research has shown the isoflavone daidzein may help stop the loss of calcium, a preventive measure against osteoporosis.

September
Yoga Parties

At the time of the Autumn Equinox, September 22, signs are present everywhere that nature is turning inward. Take this visible change in the world as your invitation also to turn inward and reflect.

One way to do this for yourself and others is to host a private yoga party. Call a local yoga studio or gym and hire an instructor. Turn one of your larger rooms into a temporary yoga studio: create a peaceful sanctuary with soft music (without lyrics). Either dim the lights or light several candles around the room. Add a mood fragrance with pure incense such as sandalwood, cedarwood, or frankincense, and roll out the sticky mats.

At the door, greet your fellow yogis with instructions to remove their shoes, enter the yoga room in silence, and sit in a comfortable position on the mat. Under the instructor's gentle guidance, be introduced to a new way of moving, thinking, and being still and quiet.

Spinach Fruit Salad by Mary Alice Page-Allen
   8 cups fresh spinach
   1 orange, peeled
   1 apple, cored and sliced
   1 cup strawberries
   1 cup kiwi, peeled and sliced
   1/4 cup walnut pieces
Dressing: Whisk together 3/4 cup strawberry yogurt with 3 tbsp. raspberry vinegar and 1/2 tsp. dried basil.

Mix spinach and fruit together in a bowl. Sprinkle walnuts on top. Serve dressing on the side.

Together, learn the importance and benefits of deep belly breathing, experience how stretching will open the body to better health and vigor, and recognize that this is exactly what the mind, body, and spirit need to be replenished. The asanas (poses) will help you see what is possible. Take the practice home with you—this wonderful new way of living can be part of every day.

Afterward, share a healthy lunch with lots of water. *Namasté*.

October
Private Spa Days

Once a year, treat yourself, your mother, your sister(s), and your best friends to a luxurious trip to the closest spa destination—your house.

Unpack the footbath and the wax-paraffin machine, mix an oatmeal and honey facial mask, and slice some cucumbers. Play the soothing, soft music frequently heard at the local spa—call them for suggestions and make the purchase in honor of this reserved time.

Part of the fun is the research and shopping for ingredients. There are many books available on how to make facial masks and mix soothing massage-oil blends. Let research be part of your preparty fun—assign a different recipe to each participant.

Give each other manicures and pedicures—don't forget the hand and foot massages, too. This relaxing party

> *Permission to Pamper:* Meet your spa friends at a local nail salon and bask in the luxury of a French manicure together.

> Play the soothing meditative music heard at many spas, such as that by the new young recording artist Evren Ozan, who won the 2001 Native American Music Awards for his CD *As Things Could Be*.

is particularly magnificent when thrown in the dead of winter. Be sure to use tropical hand lotions and bring home the aromas of the islands.

Remember to offer your spa patrons a special beverage, such as iced herbal tea served with an orange slice.

One year prior to the busy holiday season, my daughter and I invited other mothers and their daughters to join us in bathrobes and slippers for a relaxing spa morning. We made an almond-honey facial scrub and tested an apple-banana mask. We soothed our eyes with cucumber slices and soaked our tired feet in warm footbaths. Mothers painted their daughters' fingernails and vice versa and talked about big and little issues that mattered. The group also tried to be still and quiet and relax awhile.

Afterward, with shiny new skin and happy hands and feet, we savored tall, frosted virgin piña coladas complete with pineapple spears and Japanese paper umbrellas.

November
Tea Party
November, with its chilly afternoons and early darkening skies, is a perfect reason to set off on an adventure of tea exploration. Start shopping in October to ensure your private tea-tasting parties can begin on November first. Loose-leaf tea is available in sample-sized packets at teahouses, on the Internet, and via direct-mail catalogs.

Use your teatime to be reflective. Be still and quiet as you wait for the water to boil and for the tea to steep—no phone calls or magazines. Your body, mind, and spirit need this serenity to fill yourself back up after giving to your family, job, other

> **If you are cold, tea will warm you—if you are too heated, it will cool you—if you are depressed, it will cheer you—if you are excited, it will calm you.**
> —William Gladstone
> (1809–1898)

> **Serenity is a gift from you to you.**
> —Dorothy Briggs (b. 1924)

relationships, and charitable causes. Give yourself what you deserve—time alone—frequently and without guilt or needing permission.

Whether your tea parties are for one or many, decide to circumnavigate the globe from your homeport. Post a map of the world in your newly designated tearoom. Use straight pins with different metallic-colored tops and white stickers or slips of paper to mark where your trip has taken you so far. As you sip and sample your newest discovery from a distant land, pinpoint this bountiful ground on your map. At the end of the month, you will feel as if you have traveled the world simply by tasting its most popular beverage.

Later in the month, when you want the company of gregarious others, invite them to share in this adventure. Call other mothers, mother-and-daughter pairs, a new or old-time neighbor, a business acquaintance, or your very best friend to join you on your tea-tasting journey around the world.

In a study reported in the January 2003 issue of *Preventive Medicine*, six cups of black tea a day lowered the risk of heart disease by more than 50 percent. Black tea, loaded with antioxidant flavonoids, reduces the chance of stroke, clotting, and hardening of the arteries.

Permission to Travel: Add the Boulder, Colorado, Dushanbe Tea House to your list of places to visit. With more than one hundred teas on its menu, along with wonderful vegetarian dishes, this detour is definitely worth it.

According to a recent article in *Yoga Journal*, "More tea is drunk worldwide than any other beverage except water."

Try a pot of the new herbal red tea from South Africa or the south of China. Its small, mahogany-colored berries do not look like tea at all, but one taste and it might become your new favorite. It is equally as good served iced for those who already have a lot of fire in their spirit.

Next, proceed to a "white" tea, which is actually a green tea. Its knobby, clear needles (leaves) produce a delicious, pale liquid. After comparing this cup to other green teas, oolong, and black teas, you will know why white tea has been bestowed with the title of "the champagne of teas."

If tea becomes a passion in your days, why not set up a tearoom? Prowl antique shops or garage sales for unique teacups and saucers. Visit teahouses to borrow ideas for your new room, or peruse tea books for serving ideas and new recipes.

December
Personal Spaces

The ancient Indian practice of *vastu* suggests creating a tranquility zone for your spirit. This is a place to find peace whenever you simply look at this space. In your office or home, include visual treats, eye candy, to make you smile every time you see it. It could be framed drawings by your children or grandchildren, a pressed blossom, a piece of sculpture you made yourself or bought from a budding young artist, or a beautiful object found in nature.

This month, decide to throw a party for someone who deserves it the most—you. Within the next thirty days, design your own space within your home, or, if it already exists, enhance it by layering treats for the five senses therein. Bring tactile comforts such as soft blankets and huge fluffy pillows. Use aromatherapy to stimulate creativity or calm your spirit and soothing music to soothe your tired body and mind. As author and artist Julia Cameron said, "Pampering myself will make me strong."

If you like to write, create a writing studio and claim the space as yours. Visit it to pen happy letters, send good wishes, write in your journal, or work on your novel.

If rest is what your mind and body needs, set up a hammock and call it your nap sanctuary.

Love to read? Pick any corner and reserve it solely for this activity of escaping to other people's worlds through a good work of fiction.

Decorate your space any way you want. Fill it with new items or old, tattered ones you cherish. Go there regularly and be surrounded by what makes and keeps you unique.

> *Clip-art Idea:* Thanks to the aspiring artist in my household—my daughter—I have a constant source of inspiration. I rotate her new drawings and paintings on a series of clipboards that line my office wall...I just keep adding the new artwork and smile every time I see it.

Merry Moments

No excuses—we all need to celebrate, to have an event to look forward to each and every month. A celebration of life can be a boisterous party for many or a quiet moment of reflection reserved just for you.

Pick and choose from this chapter, rearrange ideas, borrow any of the many reasons to host a party—or be brave and invent your own. Mark the name of your event on the calendar in ink and dedicate this time to making others—and especially yourself—laugh and smile. Begin celebrating this month and next and the next...it is an easy habit to start and continue. Your friends and family will be glad you did. And you know what? So will you.

> **The aim of life is to live, and to live means to be aware, joyously, drunkenly, serenely, divinely aware.**
> —*Henry Miller (1891–1980)*

> **One must still have chaos in oneself to be able to give birth to a dancing star.**
> —*Friedrich Wilhelm Nietzsche (1844–1900)*

chapter 4

how the world CELEBRATES

*carnivals, festivals, and other excuses

A kitchen condenses the universe.
—*Betty Harper Fussell (b. 1927)*

This is your invitation to enter the kitchens of our sisters around the world. Step into their environments and learn from them. Intermingle their old-world traditions and recipes with your taste and lifestyle to discover fresh party ideas and more reasons to celebrate. This new-found fund of culinary inspiration is available to all of those willing to taste and appreciate something new.

In your search to stir up something new for your next party, travel the world through cookbooks and go on your excursion with open eyes and ears. Discover the culinary treasures that the world has to offer. For a different spin on the same old meal Thursday night or to revive a party theme, mix and match distant cultures' habits and traditions with American protocol.

You might never know what will come home with you until you explore—from unusual patterned linens, intriguing music, fascinating recipes, and sources for exotic ingredients to a new attitude about celebrating. Your kitchen and parties will never be the same again.

French Lessons

From illegal cheeses, questionable fungi hunted by pigs, and snails swimming in butter and garlic to the sautéed frog legs found on many French menus, our French sisters definitely know how to stir up the dinner table conversation. Take a tip from them the next time you ponder how to wake up your guests' palates.

The French will only eat gourmet food, good food that takes time to prepare and deserves to be enjoyed slowly, in small portions, not wolfed down with a soda. In France, lunchtime is to be savored. Maybe we could afford to learn from the French about parties and everyday celebrations.

> Tomatoes and oregano make it Italian; wine and tarragon make it French. Sour cream makes it Russian; lemon and cinnamon make it Greek. Soy sauce makes it Chinese; garlic makes it good.
> —Alice May Brock (b. 1941)

> According to www.eatbug.com, there are 1,462 known species of edible insects. Admittedly it's an acquired taste, but adding 100 grams of crickets to your diet will provide 121 calories, 12.9 grams of protein, and 5.5 grams of fat.

> France has found a unique way of controlling its unwanted critter population. They have done this by giving unwanted animals like snails, pigeons, and frogs fancy names, thus transforming common backyard pets into expensive delicacies. These are then served to gullible tourists, who will eat anything they can't pronounce.
> —Chris Harris (b. 1948)

The wild fungi known as truffles are commonly found at the roots of beech and oak trees in the Périgord region of southern France and parts of central Italy. Trained dogs or pigs are used to find this luxury food. Considered a delicacy, many regard their hunting grounds a secret.

> *Non ut edam vivo,*
> *sed vivam edo.*
> I do not live to eat,
> but eat to live.
> —*Marcus Fabius Quintilianus*
> *(c. 35–c. 95 AD)*

To date, approximately 120,000 species of mushrooms have been recorded; yet only 1,814 are recognized as edible. A wise chef always consults a professional when harvesting mushrooms or purchases these wildlife treasures from an accredited market.

If truffle hunting with a pig and eating fungi seems too chancy, then default to your local *fromagerie*. Go home happy with a thick slice of Roquefort to crumble in your Cobb salad or a small container of Gorgonzola to top your spinach salad and call each celebration with these moldy wonders a party for one or the entire clan.

> How do you govern a
> country that has 246
> varieties of cheese?
> —*Charles de Gaulle (1890–1970)*

The French regard cheese as their national specialty—in particular, Camembert. At last count, this country, roughly the size of Texas, boasted at least 365 different kinds for the tasting.

The French have perfected the art of cheese to its highest level, but at least half of these scrumptious pleasures are unavailable in the United States. For example, a little round orange bundle called *Epoisses de Bourgogne* is rare, expensive (of course), and illegal in America (raw-milk, unpasteurized cheese is not authorized for our cheese trays in any of the fifty states).

However, all is not lost. For your next wine-and-cheese party, now you have a reason to trek all over the French countryside on your quest for illegal cheese. Keep in mind that according to the French, the worse the cheese smells, the better it tastes. Share this gem of knowledge with your guests prior to presenting the cheese trays. The French will admit this is indeed a difficult concept for Americans to accept, let alone swallow.

> **In water one sees one's own face but in wine one beholds the heart of another.**
> —*French proverb*

However, if you know a few true cheese *aficionados,* or those inclined to be gastronomically adventurous, and you are fortunate enough to have a wonderful *fromagerie* (cheese shop) nearby owned by an equally wonderful *fromager* (cheese shop owner), then by all means host such a tasting party.

Bon appetit!

Cheese Tips: Rotate trays of soft, semi-hard, and hard cheese with water crackers and fruit to cleanse the palate between bites.

Greetings from Asia

From your kitchen, explore Asian cuisine. This trek can encompass fascinating dishes, party themes, and decorating ideas from Cambodia, Burma, India, Korea, Thailand, Vietnam, and China. Check out picture cookbooks from your local

International Policy: The Chinese do not eat food with hands or flatbread. It is considered to be extremely impolite, unsanitary, and uncivilized.

library or scour the Internet for intriguing ingredients and then surprise the crew this weekend with a whole new appreciation of Far East culture and its cuisine.

Japanese Lessons

In Japan, the entire meal, with the exception of dessert, is generally served all at once on a lacquered, wooden tray. Guests are encouraged to eat a little from each dish, finishing their soup and rice last. Dessert can be either a cup of *bancha* (brown twig tea) or *ryokucha* (green leaf tea) with a light, sweet dessert or piece of fruit such as orange sections or a few grapes—usually *kyoho*, a very sweet, juicy, rich purple fruit. Look for these sweet treats at your grocery store.

Follow the lead of the Japanese and invite your intimate party of several couples over for a unique dinner. String up the paper lanterns; roll out the sushi mats as placemats on the trays and add chopsticks. (If short on trays, borrow.) Ask your guests to leave their shoes at the door. You may want to provide them with slippers, as is customary.

> My doctor told me to stop having intimate dinners for four. Unless there are three other people.
> —Orson Welles (1915–1985)

Begin your meal with the Japanese expression, *"Itadakimasu!"* meaning "We are going to receive the meal!"

At the conclusion of your Japanese meal, thank the host in Japanese with the common expression: *"Gochisosama,"* which means "I have feasted."

Serve your meal portioned into small bowls and on small plates. This encourages eating smaller portions, and when the food is presented in this manner, you do not feel cheated. Your eyes as well as your taste buds get to feast on the presentation, which provides enough time also to savor good conversation among good friends.

Adopt the habit of using chopsticks and learn how to eat slower. A Japanese meal is relaxed on etiquette, especially when you consider it is accepted to slurp your soup or noodles and burp out loud at the dinning table. However, do not stand chopsticks in your rice bowl or spear your food, and avoid pointing your chopsticks at someone when you speak. Above all, do not lick them.

> The only problem with eating Italian food is that five or six days later you're hungry again.
> —George Miller (b. 1945)

Chopsticks originated in China during the Sang Dynasty (1766–1122 BC) as a substitute for knives at the table. According to Confucius, knives were equated with acts of aggression and should not be used to dine.

After spending some time in a *mukimono* class, your new knife handling techniques will be sharp. Wow your friends and turn a carrot into a double petal cup or carve a rose in full bloom from a beet, turnip, or rutabaga. Beginners can carve any of the various sizes of citrus fruits—a lemon, orange, or grapefruit—and add homemade sorbet, or carve any type of melon for the pretty bowl that your fruit salad deserves.

The Japanese word *mukimono* means to slice something.

International Seafood Lessons

Cioppino, *bouillabaisse*, and *zuppa di pesca* (depending on whether the stew was made on Spanish, French, or Italian shores) were originally known as the fisherman's dish. In many seaports, at the close of market each day the least desirable, leftover fish were cooked in a large cauldron on the beach. While ingredients varied, shellfish was the common denominator.

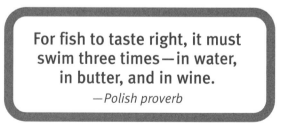

> For fish to taste right, it must swim three times—in water, in butter, and in wine.
> —Polish proverb

In some recipes, olive oil was mandatory; other ingredient lists included pepper, saffron, or dried orange zest. This hearty seafood stew can be found in almost any seaport town as part of its standard, yet much loved, cooking repertoire. So in your world travels to foreign lands or to seaside restaurants within the United States, sample a bowl here and there, and be the judge of which fishermen got the recipe just right.

For your next Mexican affair, try your hand at creating a fantastic flower from a large Spanish onion. However, if your first attempts are like mine, at least you will have enough of the onion chopped up to make salsa. If you still need a centerpiece, just place a sombrero in the center of the table.

The Calendar of Time

Pay no attention to what the calendar says here in the United States. You can use any country's carnival, festival, or excuse for a party. In fact, whereas almost every country uses the Gregorian calendar for business and government purposes, the world of traditions runs on its own clock.

Many honored agricultural festivals generally rotated around the harvest of a crop, be it blueberries, apples, or hops. *Oktoberfest* originally announced the successful harvest of hops in Munich, Germany.

On the coasts, the success of a timely bounty such as crabs, shrimp, salmon, or oysters called for a celebration. Today, the tradition continues as many cities honor their prized cash crop with huge parties lasting all day Saturday, all weekend, or even all week.

In Cambodia, Laos, and Thailand, the months are only referred to by a number.

Since the 1950s, the town of Castroville, California, attracts thousands every May to its "Choke Fest," or Artichoke Festival, to taste featured dishes, and enter or bear witness to its annual AGROart, a three-dimensional fruit and vegetable competition.

Happy New Year

The dawning of a new year is celebrated worldwide, but in each country's unique style and in some cases, on their own date. Take a look through other cultures' timetables to widen your perspective of what is possible for a celebration if you toss aside our Gregorian calendar.

> The Jewish religion recognizes Rosh Hashanah, which usually falls in September, as the start of the New Year.

The Buddhist calendar, followed by practicing Theravada Buddhists in Southeast Asia, calculates the new year based on the sun's position and the phases of the moon, related to the twelve segments of heaven, each named for a sign of the zodiac. The first day of their New Year is figured sometime between April 13 and 18 when the sun enters the segment called Aries.

The Chinese calendar is also based on lunar and solar movements. Since a lunar cycle is about twenty-nine and a half days, an extra month is added once every few years to catch up with the solar calendar (which our calendar handles by adding an extra day in a leap year). Chinese New Year's Day starts with the new moon on the first day of the year and ends with the full moon fifteen days later, when lantern-carrying children parade in a Lantern Festival.

"Gong Xi Fa Cai," **means "Celebrate, Make Money" in Chinese. Family members give red packets of lucky money, present oranges as gifts for good fortune, and ward off evil spirits with exploding firecrackers.**

There are several Hindu calendars with months ranging in length from twenty-seven to thirty-one days. New Year's Day is on several different days throughout the area. The people of Punjab and Bengal celebrate mid-April. November first or *Divali* is New Year's Day in parts of northern India; and in Nepal, it is the first day of *Vaisakha* or the April/May month.

Since the Prophet Muhammad only recognized *Eid al-Fitr* (a three-day celebration which ends Ramadan, the daylight hours fasting tradition), and *Eid al-Adha* (the Feast of Sacrifice), these are the only holidays observed by Muslims.

Once again, party people that they were, the Romans determined the very first New Year's Day in 153 BC. However, during the Middle Ages, the Christians changed it to December 25 and then later moved this celebratory date to March 25 to coincide with the Annunciation. Finally, Pope Gregory set his calendar and everyone else's in the Christian world to denote January 1 as the new year's first day once again.

The Islamic calendar only has 354 days and is completely lunar.

February
Carnival or Shrove Tuesday

This Christian tradition has inspired carnivals all over the world. Particularly well known and attended are those in New Orleans and Rio de Janeiro, Brazil. Brazil-

> Since Carnival always fell on a Tuesday, the French called it *Mardi Gras*, or Fat Tuesday.

ians celebrate Carnival as a major holiday, spending months learning songs and *samba* dances for the parades. The colored bead necklaces, lavish costume parades, and confetti have come to be known as Carnival, a derivative of the Latin *carnem levare* or *carnelevarium*, which means the removal of meat. During the Middle Ages, the tradition of celebrating carnival originated because all the meat, butter, and eggs in the house needed to be eaten on the day prior to Lent. Most people made pancakes and ate many; thus started the tradition of indulgence on the last Tuesday of February.

In England, this day is known as "Shrove Tuesday" because it is when people go to church to "shrove," or confess their sins. A story from Olney, England, inspired a new tradition that can still be witnessed around the world. In 1445, a woman was making pancakes when the shriving bell rang, so she ran to the church carrying her skillet. Ever since, the town has commemorated her dash with an official pancake race.

At this annual race, the participant is required to flip a pancake three times in her skillet in a dash to the church. Sounds like a good excuse for a little exercise and a pancake breakfast. Talk to your church about endorsing such family fun and starting a new hometown tradition.

> Germans consider their days of Carnival, or *Fastnacht*, "the eve of the fast," as the fifth season of the year in addition to the seasonal passing of time: spring, summer, autumn, winter, and *Fastnacht*.

Carnival Lamayote

In Haiti, the locals consider *Carnival Lamayote* the biggest holiday of the year. Costumes are designed as early as October. *Lamayotes*, created by the Haitian boys, are wooden or cardboard boxes decorated with paint and tissue paper. However, inside the box a "monster" is placed (your choice of a lizard, mouse, or bug). When it's time for the party, costumed participants circulate through the streets, displaying their monsters for those who'll pay a penny.

So this autumn when the weather turns nasty and keeps you indoors, entertain your kids with this story as you unwrap the art supplies. This project will keep them busy right up to early February. Then don your festive masks and costumes and parade with your *Lamayotes*. Allow only those who pay a penny (ask for fifty cents) to peek inside.

March
Holi

In India, children and adults note the coming spring harvest by throwing colored powders and water at each other. The result is a crowd covered in the colors of spring: pink, yellow, orange, and purple. This daytime, contemporary interpretation of an old-world belief dates back to when the evil witch Holika was burned. On the eve of Holi, the people lit bonfires to keep her away. Today, they celebrate in color.

Welcome spring to your neighborhood with a vast rainbow of color. The way to get everyone to come outdoors once again just might be a body-painting party. Give kids and adults alike nontoxic paints, wax pencils, and crayons designed for body art. Hire an artist to do the more decorative face designs, but allow everyone to paint everyone else's legs, arms, backs—you get the picture. Make sure that you have a camera handy.

April
Earth Month
Earth Day is celebrated around the world as a way of acknowledging our home planet and raising awareness about taking care of it. Celebrate on the designated date, April 22, or take the whole month and do thirty good deeds. Plant a tree, a flower garden, or an herb garden. Help start a beautification program in your town. Start recycling, reusing, and reducing waste at your home and office. Take mass transit to work today, ride your bike, or car pool. Yes, one person can make a difference. Give it a try and then take the credit. It will do the earth and you a world of good.

Can you think of something that can help make the world a healthier place to live? Write an editorial and send it to the local paper or contact your congressional representative by email, and let your voice and good ideas be heard.

May
May Day
Historically celebrated in Europe for centuries, May Day marked the time of year when the herds and flocks were moved to their summer grazing grounds. The tradition continues today in towns and villages throughout Europe, where people rise early in the morning to "bring in the May." The main event takes place around a maypole, which can reach

more than one hundred feet high. Dancers hold the streamers that fall from the top of the pole, and as they circle around it, the patterns are woven tighter. There is the crowning of a May Queen and much dancing and feasting into the night.

June
Midsommar

In the far north country of Sweden, the *midsommar* festival is celebrated on the longest day of the year—which is very long, as the sun sets for only a few minutes in the wee hours! Everything—cars, houses, farms, ships, trains, buses, and public buildings—is decorated with flowers, birch twigs, and garlands. People dress up in traditional costumes and dance all "night."

Does your crowd like to dance—or do they need lessons? Look up the local dance studio and request help at your midsummer festival. Kids and adults can welcome summer together and add a few new dance steps to their repertoire. Party stores, costume-rental shops, and a music store with ethnic dance songs will make your party a success. Start planning now!

Shrimp Festivals

For centuries, fishermen of the town of Oostduinkerke, Belgium, rode horses to catch shrimp. With nets dragged behind the horses, the mounted fishermen would ride into the North Sea one hour prior to the turning of the tides to bring home the bounty. Each year, seaside festivals begin with a children's fishing competition, a sea parade (yes, through the tides), and an honorary ball.

Oceanfront feasts originated with the Wampanoag and other Native Americans from Cape Cod to Allen's Neck, Massachusetts. Today along any North American coast, time-honored ritual feasts are celebrated, such as clam-bakes, crayfish boils, lobster bakes, and shrimp fests.

For equestrian families, this may be a new entertainment at your family gatherings. If you live seaside, mark a date in late June for your next shrimp boil. Encourage the kids or feisty adults to organize a parade at the edge of the sea as tradition dictates. Hold your party on the beach and raise your cups in a toast to the brave Belgian fishermen of yesteryear. If land-locked, that is still no excuse to miss this shrimp festival. Stoke up the barbeque, turn up the music, and celebrate with the faraway residents of Oostduinkerke.

July
Lobster Carnival

Food, especially seafood, has always been a good reason for a party. Here's another occasion to add to your list: Join the good people of Pictou, Nova Scotia, in celebrating the end of their fishing season. You can either go to Canada and celebrate with the locals or recreate a lobster carnival at home. To follow tradition, you will need a female band donning traditional Scottish kilts and performing on bagpipes. You will eat lobster all day long and watch skilled competitors shell lobsters and tie ropes for the traps. (You may need to import this attraction.) And as with all good carnivals, there must be a parade and the evening must end with Highland dancing in the streets.

Your neighbors will talk for years about this one...so you may want to invite them.

Tanabata

In Japan, on the seventh day of the sebenth month, it is an annual summer tradition to write your wishes on paper and hang the messages from bamboo branches. Also called the Star Festival, this event is based on the Chinese legend of two lovers being separated by the Milky Way and meeting only once a year on this date in July. Reconstruct the event in your own backyard—festoon the trees and then go around and read the messages from your loved ones.

August
Eisteddfod Genedlaethol

For those blessed with the writing gene, the Welsh have a good idea to try. Celebrate in August with this group of fun-loving people and try your hand at penning a poem in

Famous Poets in Your Family?
- *Irish:* Paula Meehan, Mary O'Malley, Eavan Boland, Medbh McGuckian
- *English:* Elizabeth Barrett Browning, Charlotte Turner Smith, Mary Robinson, Joanna Baillie
- *Italian:* Mariella Bettarini, Gabriella Leto, Piera Oppezzo
- *German:* Helga M. Novak, Brigitte Oleschinski, Nelly Sachs
- *Spanish:* Rosalía de Castro, Carmen Conde, Francisca Aguirre, Ana Rossetti
- *Japanese:* Yosano Akiko, Okamoto Kanoko, Okuhara Seiko, Hashimoto Takako
- *Chinese:* Li Qingzhao, Zhu Shuzhen, Kimiko Hahn,
- *French:* Louise Ackerman, Adélaïde Dufrénoy, Marie Krysinska, Amable Tastu

Laughter is the brightest in the place where food is.
—*Irish proverb*

traditional Welsh verse. The entire Welsh literary competition is a step back in time. The contestants enter the great hall wearing Druidic robes of green, white, and blue; trumpets blare and children sing. Make sure that you have all the necessary props, including someone who can read Welsh.

If there are no Welsh men or women in your family, then default to your heritage and attempt to do justice to those earlier poets of your clan. Rent regal robes for the brave participants, hire the children to play whatever instruments they know, and sit back for a rowdy time. Points may be given for presentation over writing style.

Yam Festival

Food is always a good excuse for a party, as the Ewe people of Ghana obviously agree. With dancing and drumming in every town, they celebrate the humble yam with a weeklong festival. The local priest prepares a purification bundle with a shoot of oil palm, a bush rope, and branches of the *atizdize* tree. At night when all the lights of the town go out, the procession heads out of town to bury the bundle with prayers that no evil will cross it.

The following morning, the field workers pick the new yam crop and bring the harvest into town with a big parade. The yams are tasted as the New Year begins.

If feeling blue in anticipation of the United States's New Year's Eve being more than four months away, join the Ewe people and serve yams in as many dishes as you can tonight. Pull out the fireworks, too, and wish them a "Happy New Year" from the other side of the earth.

September
Bruegel Feesten
Better than any other artist, Belgian Pieter Bruegel the Elder captured the life and times of sixteenth-century Europe in his detailed paintings. To honor him, every two years on the second Sunday of September the people of Wingene, Belgium, recreate this place in time. They dress like the people in his paintings. They play the games that he illustrated. Afterward, at his honorary banquet, the town folk act out the proverbs that he loved and serve his favorite foods: sausages, pancakes, and beer.

Pageant of the Masters
In Laguna Beach, California, every summer now for seventy years talented wizards (makeup artists and art directors) accept the challenge of recreating famous masterpieces of art on stage with live people in the Pageant of the Masters. Each subject in the painting is dressed in period clothing, painted, dusted, and lit appropriately to simulate what looks to be a larger-than-life replica of the painting or, in some cases, the sculpture. As the crowd sits spellbound, waiting for an actor to sneeze or breathe, the stage lights slowly rise, revealing the people who make the three-dimensional painting. This incredible evening under the stars is one celebration of the arts that you do not want to miss. If planning to visit Southern California, be sure to get tickets in advance.

October
Exaltation of the Shellfish
On the fourth Sunday of October, the sixteenth-century town of Grove, Spain, pays tribute to its fishing industry with a lively parade. After mass, the townspeople dress in costumes to sing and perform Galician dances called *muñeiras*. Huge baskets of live shellfish are offered at special low prices throughout this northwestern province of Pontevedra. Visitors and locals alike indulge in the delicacies from the sea.

Han-gul
In 1446, King Sejong the Great of Korea issued a proclamation, giving his people a new alphabet with twenty-four letters. Prior to this time, Koreans had used Chinese characters, which they felt did not accurately reflect the sound of their language.

> One of my favorite one-dish meals is Spain's national treasure—*paella*—steaming with lobster, clams, mussels, and shrimp, all tossed lightly in seasoned long-grain rice.

On this October holiday schools are closed and calligraphy contests are held for children and adults alike with very large cash prizes awarded to the best.

Be inspired to begin your own alphabet, or at least give the kids a day off from school to learn about another culture. Consider this time spent with them a field trip to a foreign land without the required passport, immunization shots, and currency exchange.

Make a day of the *Han-gul* celebration. Create a typical Korean breakfast of *kimch'l* (a spicy pickled vegetable soup), rice, smoked meat, and tea, or pancakes made with scallions and octopus, and *bebimpop* (rice, vegetables, and lots of spices mixed together in a bowl). Note you will also need to sit cross-legged on mats at a low table, wearing no shoes. Follow breakfast with calligraphy lessons. The easiest way to practice writing these elegant characters is to use sand and the wrong end of a paintbrush.

November
Divali

In India, it is believed that on the day of *Divali*, the Hindu goddess of wealth and prosperity, Lakshmi, visits every home in the nation. Families clean and whitewash their houses and brush colored powder on their floors to create paintings. Rows of little clay lamps line their court-yard walls, windowsills, and rooftops. In Hindu, *Divali* means a row of lights. It is believed that if a house (or business) is not lit up, Lakshmi will not visit and bless its inhabitants.

Instead of spring cleaning, why not institute autumn cleaning—just in time for the holidays. Promise the troops a special dinner celebration, dinner, bath, and stories by candle-light if all is done before party time. You might want to skip the painting on the floors of your house, but adapt the idea to play with sidewalk chalk or draw on large sheets of paper.

Wan Loy Kratong

For approximately seven thousand years, the "Festival of the Floating Leaf Cups" has been cel-ebrated in Thailand at the first full moon of November. On this day little boats, or *kratongs,* are made out of lotus, banana leaves, or paper in the shape of a cup, animal, or temple.

Inside the boats, a candle, incense, and a coin or gardenias are placed. By moonlight, the families make a wish and release their boats. If the candle stays lit until the *kratong* dis-appears, the wish that was made upon the launch will come true.

This November, bring this tradition to your family and try your hands at making *kra-tongs.* After a special meal together spent discussing the trials and tribulations of your boat crafting, head to the closest river. Not available within driving distance? Make your own river using your garden hose in the street.

December
Night of the Radishes (La Noche de Rabaños)

Around the city of Oaxaca, Mexico, radishes grow so large that sometimes they measure the length of a child's arm. This city's annual radish-sculpture competition draws many artists, who come to carve images of public figures, familiar landmarks, or Christmas scenes. The best entry wins a prize, and all are displayed in the town square.

Luciadagen

The Scandinavian celebration of St. Lucia of Sicily bestows to the oldest girl in the family the duty of serving coffee and saffron buns to all the adults while wearing the traditional garb of a white robe tied with a red sash and atop her head, a crown of burning white candles. The other children, also dressed in traditional clothing, follow her.

On my husband's side of the family, we celebrate the festival of Lucia in a similar fashion. However, the crown the eldest wears is made of candles with battery-operated flames instead—and we dance. For a month prior to the date, six couples get together to either relearn or learn the dance steps. We enjoy the practice sessions almost as much as the occasion when all eyes are watching. Between dance performances, traditional cookies and sweets along with special regional dishes are presented for nibbling.

Kulig

After a deep snowfall, it is a Polish tradition to take friends on a horse-drawn sleigh ride for the *Kulig*—a winter sleigh party. During the ride to the party spot, firecrackers are thrown and children tumble in the snowdrifts. When a suitable spot is found in the forest, a fire is made and a hearty supper is prepared. Afterward, there is much dancing—probably to stay warm.

Traditionally, one travels house to house, where friends are awakened to eat and drink and join the growing party.

How to say Bon Appétit:
Danish: *Velbekomme*!
German: *Guten appetit!*
Italian: *Buon appetito!*
Japanese: *Itadakimas!*
Lithuanian: *Skanaus!*
Persian: *Noosh-e jan!*
Spanish: *¡Buen provecho!*
Swedish: *Smaklig måltid!*
English: Enjoy your meal!

chapter 5

life's
MILESTONES

*precious moments

Nothing is too wonderful to be true.
—Michael Faraday (1791–1867)

Milestones celebrated during a lifetime—whether for friends, family, and ourselves—are about growth, commitment, renewal, and rebirth. As we follow the timeline of life, there are certain moments that will forever stand out from the average day. From the birth of a child or the celebration of a "sweet sixteen" birthday party to graduations, weddings, promotions, and retirements—how can we make these times count for the honored guest or ourselves?

We need to approach the celebration of an upcoming milestone with thought and conviction—not always with expensive, catered dinners and reactionary, big-ticket gifts. With a little foresight and creative brainstorming, a grand event or gift can be both simple and great without spending a fortune.

But what to give to show we care? How about special treatment, words of encouragement, compliments, unconditional love, a day off from the regular grind, or time reserved for priceless moments together?

We also need to find new ways to celebrate what is sometimes painful in our lives: birthdays (yes—each and every one of them) as well as the passing of a loved one.

How do we acknowledge the monumental moments in a young person's life? What do we do in America when a girl becomes a woman? Is there a celebration when a teenager passes her driver's test or just warnings issued to the neighbors to "clear the streets"?

What can we do to emphasize the important decision when a young adult accepts the responsibility of the right to vote? Can we, as parents and a society, establish a meaningful ritual for a young person when he or she officially becomes an adult at the age of twenty-one—without alcohol?

Honor your life's milestones, moments important to you. Create your own mother-daughter celebrations, husband-and-wife quarterly outings, or big family get-togethers. Pick a date, make the calls, and come together "just because." In the company of good friends, the reasons to enjoy life will present themselves.

Happy Birthday!

Birthdays parties began in Europe a long time ago when people believed evil spirits gravitated toward the celebrant on their birthdays. To counter the evil spirits, they surrounded the birthday person with good thoughts, wishes, and presents. Traditionally, only kings celebrated, but eventually the first children's birthday parties were celebrated in Germany and called *kinderfests*.

Name Day, instead of a birthday, is celebrated in many countries, including Finland, Bulgaria, Greece, Poland, Russia, Sweden, and Lithuania. In the early days of Christianity, Name Days were observed as Saint's Day. In the Czech Republic, any woman named Olga celebrates on the eleventh of July. In Finland, one week of July is called "women's week" because it is the week for those with the names: Riikka, Saara, Marketta, Johnanna, Leena, and Kristiina.

Here in the States, birthdays—at least during childhood—are a big deal for many. Unfortunately, as a little girl ages, she seems to have two choices. She can resort to being either "twenty-nine forever" or elect to ignore this annual milestone in the passage of time.

I completely disagree with both options. In fact, I make it a point to tell the world my age—much to the chagrin of several of my friends who are also my age.

Birthdays should be a day of freedom to reflect, contemplate, or explore life's possibilities. The celebrant should be empowered to reach for the future, embrace it with both arms, and see all that is possible—not mourn the passing of another year.

On traditional "over-the-hill" birthdays, forget the black balloons, the wheelchair or walker, geriatrics supplies, and sympathy cards. Why? While these pranks may be funny to the group, the birthday gal might be less than thrilled, and it is her day. The following are some alternative ways to create laughter and fun on her special day.

> **If I'd known I was going to live this long, I'd have taken better care of myself.**
> —*Ubie Blake (1883–1983)*

Wiggin' Birthdays

In England, my friend Hilary Jones tells of her "wiggin'" birthday celebrations where the birthday girl and her best friends don wigs and dash about town. This party concept is that everyone can be whoever she has always wanted to be on this special night—a brazen redhead, a dazzling brunette, a punk rocker with pink hair, or a blonde bombshell. The end result is hilarious hours of laughs, smiles, and fun.

On your birthday this year, wear a wig, a hat, or a costume.

The Balloon Cake

Please feel free to call this idea your own, but note that you can only do this party cake once with the same crowd. If you try to pull it off twice, especially in the same year, they will be wise to you.

For my brother-in-law's birthday, my daughter, my nieces, and I made a "ski-hill cake," since Bryon loves to ski. Decorated with plastic miniature pine trees and two tiny ski poles and skis, it did resemble one of the hills that I learned to ski on back East.

When the birthday guy cut the cake, it exploded due to the hidden element responsible for the ski hill—an inflated balloon. I never saw my mother-in-law laugh so hard.

The trick is to inflate a round balloon and cut out a large section in the center of the cake to accommodate it. One-layer cakes work best, with icing used to disguise the balloon.

Since a sharp knife will ensure the icing flies, you may want to do the cake-cutting ceremony outside. Use your imagination to build a golf hill, a garden slope, the round earth, the moon—whatever you can create with icing, food dye, a balloon, and decorations to distract from the protruding lump in the cake.

It is an exact science to get the balloon to explode and not simply lose air and collapse on itself or deflate under the weight of too much icing, and this cake does take time to perfect your cake-decorating skills. Pick

Hire "people of fun" for your birthday celebration: a fortune teller, a magician, actors, belly dancers, or singers.

Vietnam: Since the Vietnamese do not acknowledge the exact day they were born, everyone celebrates on New Year's Eve and recognizes the symbol of the lunar calendar as their sign. A baby turns one on *Tet*, the first day of the New Year, no matter when he or she was born that year. Parents congratulate their birthday child on becoming a year older and present her with a red envelope containing *li xi* or "lucky money."

your victims unrelated to each other so you can have plenty of practice, but regardless of how the cake explodes, it is always a big hit.

Celebrate Big

I believe in celebrating my birth in a big way, and encourage friends and family to help me celebrate for at least a week and some years, for the entire month. Two reasons for this lengthy celebration of life: 1) with friends and family scattered across the country, their good wishes and opportunity to celebrate with me never quite make it on the designated date, which is fine with me, and 2) the expression, "the more, the merrier," also works for the number of birthday parties that you can have in one year.

> Send a good friend who lives far away a birthday card for as many years as she has graced this earth. Start early enough to be sure that she will receive the last good wish on her actual birthday.

This year I decided, in honor of my heritage, to throw a party in true Greek fashion, complete with a belly dancer, plate breaking, festive music, and wonderful authentic food provided by my talented friends. I wanted to paint a Greek flag on the garage door, but my husband said "no," so I bought a flag instead.

I had envisioned creating a formal setting with tall tapers and white-linen–covered tables lining our long driveway; however, an afternoon thundershower, which lasted through dinner, pushed the crowd onto our covered front porch and inside to my half-finished remodeled kitchen—complete with dust, boxes, and general chaos.

When it stopped raining, the kids sold small plates for twenty-five cents for the guests to break and yell, "*Ompah*." The proceeds were donated to charity.

We shot off forty fireworks and ice blocked (slid down the grassy slope on a block of ice) until it grew too dark to see the trees at the bottom of the hill. *Ompah!*

I had to miss my father's fiftieth birthday party and felt badly about it, but I had an idea on how to be in two places at once. My husband and I dressed in our best clothes and sat at the table wearing party hats. We took photos, had them enlarged to life size, and mounted them on foam core with standup easels. I mailed them to my stepmother, who propped us up at the table as "sit ins" for us. My father knew that we wanted to be there, and at least we were there in spirit.

Host the party that you have always wished someone would throw for you. Plan it now.

It is your birthday—you set the perfect menu. What is your all-time favorite food? Should you fly lobster in from Maine? Or is your favorite seafood soft-shell blue crab from Maryland? Are your culinary preferences more along the lines of meat and potatoes? How about some smoked ribs from Texas or a baked Virginia ham? Maybe you want to eat your dessert first or only serve desserts at your party.

Eat lighter this Thanksgiving or holiday season and take some of the time, money, and energy usually spent in the last six weeks of the year to do it up for your birthday celebration.

Isn't life grand?

Steamboat Springs, Colorado: Deb Proper missed her high school prom, so for her milestone birthday she decided to host a prom party complete with a professional photographer taking portraits under the lattice archway and a theme: Moonlight Gardens. Deb, an artist, painted a mural of a moonlight garden, while friends decorated with flowers and hung silver stars from the ceiling. She asked her guests to bring their prom pictures from decades ago, which were attached to the stars. Couples arrived dressed in formal attire— today's styles as well as prom dresses from the sixties and tuxedo-printed T-shirts.

Hungarian children celebrate both their birthdays and their Name Days.

Japan: It is typical to receive a lobster on your birthday. Since the crustacean's bent back is thought to symbolize old age, its presentation is the hope for "many happy returns." Sounds to me like a good idea to host a lobster bake for a birthday party!

89

Celebrate Quietly

For your big birthday this year, or any year for that matter, maybe what you truly need is time—time alone with just you—so you can understand and appreciate the complicated, wonderful, beautiful person you are.

Your birthday deserves reflection of the past and also warrants inspection of the future. As we all write our own life story, it is important to acknowledge the past, and grow from it, or let it go, be proud of your current life, and honor yourself.

Below are a few ideas to celebrate you with just you.

> In Chinese symbolism, the sunflower represents longevity. What a perfect bouquet to give a friend who is approaching a milestone birthday.

Letters to Myself

On the eve or day of your birthday, sit down with your favorite pen and scented stationery. Write a letter to yourself. (If your handwriting is like mine, use a typewriter or the computer.) The idea behind this personal celebration is to capture a snapshot of where you are now in life and where you would like to be if there were absolutely no constraints on money or time, nor any responsibility to anyone other than yourself. Be careful of what you wish for—dreams, when written down, do have a way of coming true...

> **Love yourself first and everything else falls into line.**
> —*Lucille Ball (1911–1989)*

Whatever you write is right; the fact that you are making this time for yourself is what matters. Remember to write in the first person, use the word "I" frequently, and brag a lot. This is not the time or place for humility.

On book tour this past year, I asked women to give themselves permission to do whatever they truly wanted to do. At the conclusion of my talk, I collected their letters and sealed the envelopes with a wax stamp. In a year, I will mail them the letters so they can review the promises that they made to themselves that day.

I invite you to do the same. When your letter arrives, do not open it. Put it in a safe place as the present to be opened first on your next birthday.

Will you recognize yourself as that same woman a year later? Will you be proud of the woman you have grown to be? Will your observations from a year ago help you be kinder to yourself, more generous with time for self-care, and more appreciative of your blessed life now?

My advice is to keep all of the letters, too. After a decade (or decades), you will know how this strong, powerful, and confident woman has become who she is today.

(P.S. You can start this self-care, introspective habit anytime—just do not open your letter until your birthday.)

Wish Box

According to Scott Cunningham in his book *The Magic of Food*, the birthday candles on the cake were originally arranged to represent the celebrant's astrological sign. The act of blowing the candles out is steeped in an ancient spiritual magic with the belief that the writing on the cake contains magic, and if the cake is consumed, the wish will come true. So, it is advisable to have a birthday cake and eat a slice of your cake, too.

Since many women have chosen to nix the birthday (and birthday cake), I propose the

> **May your days be good and long upon the Earth.**
> —*Apache Blessing*

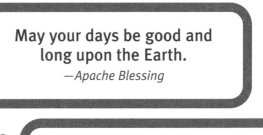

> **Why is birthday cake the only food you can blow out and spit on, and everybody wants to get a piece?**
> —*Corey Feldman (b. 1971)*
> *as Bobby Keller in Dream a Little Dream*

concept of having a "Wish Box." This is your unrestricted opportunity to wish—practical and impractical. On a separate piece of colorful paper, write each wish in gold ink. Fold each slip in half and tuck it into a small box. Wrap your wish box in fancy paper, and tie the box shut with a gorgeous ribbon.

One year from this "wish-making" ceremony, open the box and revisit your dreams. Better than a box of fortune cookies, these words of inspiration have the potential of coming true with your fortitude and tenacity.

> Tracy Stoddard, who is turning forty this year, has set the Boulder Backroads Marathon as her birthday goal. It will be the first 26.2 miles she has ever run.

Birthday Goals

Another way to "celebrate you" on this very special day is to set a challenge for yourself. With a due date for maturity very far away—in a year—anything is possible, especially if the task is divided into small steps to be accomplished over a twelve-month period. Invite a friend who is approaching the same birthday to join you. Together, you can endure any setbacks, motivate each other, and at the end—celebrate.

The only requirement is to have reached your goal prior to the next birthday. Why? Because it will be time to set a new challenge to be added to your birthday repertoire of accomplishments.

My birthday repertoire is full of adventures—from 5K races, biathlons, and triathlons; century rides and trips all across the country—things that I would never have done if I had not promised myself this birthday present of achievement. A year later, I was healthier and happier because of this achieved goal.

Happy birthday! Celebrate your day and your life.

> **The world is terrified of a joyful woman. Make a stand. Be one anyway.**
> —*Marianne Williamson (b. 1952)*

The Celebration of Girls to Women

Why is the physical change in our bodies when a young girl becomes a woman called "the curse"? This hushed topic is not spoken of nor celebrated in America the way it is in other cultures. What can be learned from the way our international sisters view this life change in girls? How can we celebrate with our daughters this important moment of becoming a woman?

There are several excellent books about how we can better understand this time in our lives and what others before us have practiced, believed, and lived. Share the ideas, thoughts, and activities from these books with the young women in your life. Make a difference in their young lives. Let them take pride in the transition to womanhood.

- *Red Moon: Understanding and Using the Gifts of the Menstrual Cycle* by Miranda Gray
- *Honoring Menstruation: A Time of Self-Renewal* by Lara Owen
- *Women's Medicine Ways: Cross-Cultural Rites of Passage* by Marcia Starck and Gynne Stern

The women of Native American societies would go to the moon hut for the time of their bleeding. Believed to be at the height of her powers, she was not to trouble herself with mundane social or sexual distractions. This was a time to be with other women and to grow spiritually stronger and wiser, concentrating on the wisdom exchanged within this intimate group.

In the historical novel, *The Red Tent*, author Anita Diamant takes one line from the Bible and creates the life and times of Dinah, one of the daughters of Jacob, and the women never spoken of in the rest of the book of Genesis. Women of

Sunrise Dance: When a girl turns fourteen among the White Mountain Apache Indians, a celebration is hosted in honor of her becoming a woman. The "Sunrise Dance" is a four-day celebration with blessings, stories, and dances. Each girl wears a buckskin dress, an eagle feather in her hair to represent long life, and on her forehead, an abalone shell to represent Changing Woman, Mother of the Apache.

this time were given a red tent when it became their time of the full moon to rest and regenerate. In this tent, they were taken care of by each other and the younger girls.

I think American women would relish the idea of three whole days each month to do absolutely nothing.

This is a time in a young girl's life when other women should rally around her and share stories of what it means to be a woman. Funny, sad, embarrassing moments—however the afternoon or evening unfolds, this transformation should not be a time of secrecy and unspoken words but an occasion of renewal, growth, and acceptance in a supportive network of her fellow female companions.

> *Gift Ideas:* Special journal and pen, luxurious bath items, satiny bathrobe, soothing music, books—fill her shelves with stories about strong women by female authors.

Throw a party, host an afternoon tea, go shopping—celebrate with your daughter, niece, or granddaughter—this should be a proud moment in her young life. Be proud to be a woman and let her know that she should be, too.

Marriage Rituals

Bridal showers were given to strengthen ties between the bride and her friends, to provide moral support, and to help her prepare for marriage. In the 1890s, the idea started to give the bride-to-be gifts. Supposedly, at one shower, friends placed small gifts inside a parasol and opened it over the bride so the presents would shower over her. This story, when picked up by a fashion magazine, had women everywhere adopting the idea as their own.

> *Bridal Showers:* According to legend, a Dutch girl became engaged to a local boy, but the girl's father looked down upon the penniless groom-to-be and would not give his approval. When the town folks heard of this misfortune, they "showered" the young couple with everything needed to start a home. In the end, the father did give his blessing.

Kim Lipker of Fort Collins suggests hosting a Wine Shower for those women who marry later, since their households are already established. The men are also invited to this shower and the couple gets their wine cellar stocked by friends and family.

My friend Alex, who is originally from England, told me that their bachlorette night is actually called "Hen night." Sometimes, she forgets where she is and asks her engaged American friends, "What are we going to do for your Hen night?" They look at her blankly until she explains.

The Naughty Bridal Shower

The emphasis of this party is to make the bride blush. Instruct all of the guests to bring a racy gift, something to keep the fires of the marriage bed hot for a very long time. This gives the invited guests an excuse to peruse a different shelf at the bookstore or visit a brand new store. If a bit shy, the Internet offers a host of props, costumes, videos, and books.

Be creative with the cake, decorations, and enforce a sexy dress code. Maybe hire a male dancer as a prelude to the gift-opening ceremony. At the end of this party, at least the bride (and groom) will have something that they can really use.

"I Do"

Traditions and customs for the union of two people have been shared, borrowed, and adopted from all over the world. Middle Eastern cultures adopted the Greek and Roman custom of the brides wearing yellow or red bridal veils (representing fire) to ward off demons. At one time in history, Roman brides were completely covered in a red veil and it was not removed until after the wedding ceremony. The Crusaders brought the bridal-veil tradition back to Europe, but changed it to white.

During the fourteenth century throughout Europe, superstitions encouraged the guests to literally take a piece of the bride's dress to bring good luck and so they ripped off pieces as she danced by or tried to escape. To prevent this destruction and protect the bride, the tradition arose of throwing various items to the guests, such as the garter belt and the bouquet.

Wedding Symbolism

In the United States, we wear our wedding rings on the fourth finger of the left hand for several reasons:

In 1449, Ann of Brittany popularized the white wedding gown. Prior to that time, the bride simply wore her best dress or a new dress without the issue of color being a factor.

The Roman explanation is that with the left hand being used less often and the fourth finger not easily extendable without the rest of the fingers, it is the finger best protected.

The Greeks and Egyptians chose the third finger because they believed it to be connected directly to the heart by a route that they called "the vein of love."

In third-century Greece, the ring finger was the index finger. In India, it was the thumb.

The Christian church, to impress the seriousness of the ceremony upon the bride and groom, told the couple the first three fingers are for the Father, the Son, and the Holy Ghost, and the fourth finger represents the earthly love of husband and wife, their marriage, and the hope of Heaven.

Traditional Traditions

Wedding traditions from around the world are steeped in religious, superstitious, and cultural differences. Add any of these practices to your wedding and see what happens:

In Wales, it is customary to kidnap the bride just before the ceremony. The groom and his family follow in pursuit. Local lore states that whoever rescues the damsel in distress will marry within a year.

A traditional Moroccan wedding lasts from four to seven days. Once the vows have been exchanged and before the bride can become the mistress of her new home, she must walk around the outside of her house three times.

In Norway, after the wedding, friends place two small pine trees on either side of the newlyweds' front door until they have a baby, at which time the trees are replanted in the yard.

The tradition of the "best man" originated among the Germanic Goths of Northern Europe in 200 AD. Whenever a man had to capture his bride from a neighboring village, the bridegroom would be accompanied by his strongest friend (or best man) who helped him capture his new wife.

In Italy, legend tells of a servant who stole a branch of jasmine to give to his bride. At this time and according to law, only the duke, the legendary Medici and his family, was allowed to grow this fragrant bloom. The couple not only secretly grew the beautiful flower, but also sold it. Today, Italian brides often wear a sprig of jasmine on their wedding day, hoping for an increase of good luck.

Traditional Cakes

At wedding receptions in Jamaica, the bridal party and guests enjoy a dark fruitcake liberally laced with rum, and a slice is mailed to those not in attendance.

In Bermuda, wedding cakes are topped with a tiny sapling. After the reception, the newlyweds plant it at their new home and watch it grow, along with their marriage.

The tradition of a groom's cake began in England and Ireland and was typically a fruitcake with white icing, served along with the wedding cake. Today, chocolate cake instead of fruitcake is served.

In first century BC Rome, a wedding cake made of wheat or barley, regarded as a symbol of fertility, was thrown at the bride or broken over her head.

Prior to good-tasting wedding cakes, the tradition was to stack several cakes atop one another as tall as possible to make the couple kiss over it without knocking it down. If they succeeded, a lifetime of good fortune was certain.

> During the reign of King Charles II of England, it became customary for cakes to be made palatable with icing.

There are numerous great books about how to have a grand wedding, a country wedding, and every type in between, so I will just note a few ways to make this day and the time leading up to the big celebration memorable and not a blur. Be sure to reserve moments of serenity between the chaos of putting together such a big event.

Here are a few tried and true suggestions:

- *Rest.* Build in rest time each day. Invite your mother or mother-in-law for a quiet cup of tea. No lists, no phones allowed—just twenty minutes to enjoy each other's company. Another day, take a walk around the old neighborhood.
- *Preserve.* Ask a sister, cousin, or good friend to document the week—candid photos of everyone are encouraged.
- *Seek simplicity.* Keep meals and snacks simple—fill up the fruit bowl and stock the refrigerator with healthy solutions to abate the munchies and thirst.
- *Ask.* Request assistance from family and friends; they will be happy to help.
- *Sleep.* Get adequate sleep the week prior to the wedding.
- *Shhh.* Find downtime for only you—soak in the tub, take a luxurious nap, read a book for pleasure, meditate, or practice yoga.

We're Pregnant!

For some women, being pregnant is a glorious time in their lives. They are proud to be carrying another living being. Others try to hide their secret as long as possible. For those expecting, "Congratulations!" Go do something crazy to remember this incredible time.

Before you know it, your baby will be driving a car. Here are some ideas to celebrate your nine months of bliss:

Baby's Home Cast Party

With the help of your partner or with other expectant mothers, make a plaster of paris cast of your belly. After the plaster dries, paint it—a mural of the places that you and your baby will go or an abstract, colorful work of art in bright hues. Remember to sign and date your masterpiece. In later years, you will be able to share your pregnancy memories with your child.

Paint Your Belly

You probably have heard of "Paint Your Own Pottery" shops—well, why not implement the idea of a "Paint Your Pregnant Belly" workshop? Invite over other mothers-to-be and get out the paintbrushes and nontoxic paints.

For a more personal interpretation, make it a private party—just you and the baby's father. Invite him to be the artist or paint together, and create a mural of beauty to share with your child later. Once again, the creation will be all yours. Remember to take photos to add to your baby's first album.

Baby Photo Shoot

Host your own photo shoot or invite other expectant mothers. Hire a professional or someone good with a camera (a tripod always helps), a makeup artist, and a hairstylist—these extras on the set could be your nonpregnant friends. Change outfits and rotate the sets. Afterward, either frame and hang the photos in your baby's room or make a pregnant photo album to share with your little one once she arrives.

The Bubble Gum Baby Game

To initiate the glowing couple into parenthood, try this co-ed baby-shower game. It is messy, gooey, and lots of fun—similar to raising a child.

Give everyone two pieces of bubble gum. Instruct the participants to chew until the gum is soft and juicy. Distribute pink or blue slips of paper roughly the size of a business card printed with this message: *This is what I think a newborn baby looks like:*

Announce a time limit of ten minutes to the new parents, experienced ones, and those completely out of their league to mold their pliable yet sticky material into their artistic interpretation. Some renditions of a newborn will be quite good, others just a blob—but either way it is all in the name of fun.

Mission Possible

Know an expectant mother? Give her closest friends and family members a disposable camera and a nine-month mission: to take twenty-seven candid shots of the mother-to-be over the term of her pregnancy.

> For a centerpiece on the tables for a baby shower, fill baby bottles with flowers and give to the expectant mother to take home afterwards.

Make sure that you have all the bases of her life covered—the gym, the mall, church, work, and anywhere else she frequents. Two weeks prior to the baby shower, develop the pictures and then have fun pulling together the progressive photo album at the party with the new mom-to-be. Encourage the detective to take notes while on assignment and include them with the photos for extra laughs. Give photo-credit lines where due.

Twenty years from now, the baby will personally thank each and every one of you for this insight into her mother.

Birthing Circle

Baby showers of the past celebrated among women in America generally provided the mother-to-be with gear. In Steamboat Springs, Colorado, a new tradition has started for expectant mothers called the birthing circle. The local bead store, The Silver Lining, helps friends of the mom-to-be choose a bead to be included on a bracelet symbolic of their emotional support.

At the private gathering, the expectant mother soaks her feet while the other women share their stories and reflections of motherhood and offer wishes to the new baby and mother as they add their bead to the bracelet. After the last rite of passage and tradition into motherhood is told, she is given the bracelet to wear until her baby is delivered. This empowering custom honors, nurtures, and pampers the mother-to-be, reminding her that she is not alone and can draw upon the strength of those women who have gone before her.

> Create your own way to comfort and honor an expectant mother. Consult *The Pregnant Women's Comfort Book* by Jennifer Louden for ideas.

Surprise!

My mother threw a surprise party for me for my sixteenth birthday—but the surprise was on those who attended. To get me out of the house so the guests could arrive, my best friend, Jennifer, took me to get my hair cut. I decided to do something drastic and chopped my long hair into a pixie. You should have seen the looks on my friends' faces (and my mother's) when I opened the front door!

Not just for birthdays anymore, you can surprise a host of people with a host of good reasons. A promotion, relocation, or a raise—all call for a grand celebration. Any accomplishment—whether it is venturing out, moving up, or retiring from a successful career and succeeding with a personal goal—should be recognized.

The toughest part, of course, is keeping the celebration a secret, but it can be done. Tell everyone, including the editor of the society pages, just not the surprise-party recipient.

Do you know a musician who has recorded a CD? Host a surprise party and bring her CD to sell at the party. Book the event at a popular restaurant and share the good news prior with the owner and the entire staff.

What about an athlete who has broken a record, professionally or personally? Dress in tacky tracksuits popular in the seventies and let this guest of honor have the entire spotlight. Present her or him with a gold pseudo-Olympic medal for tenacity and effort.

Do you know a medical or veterinarian student who has completed her degree? Now you know what to do. Invite all of her friends and some of her favorite professors to honor both the student and the teacher (pets welcome).

Know an author? Host a party to toast the monumental task of finishing a manuscript and invite all the bibliophiles that you know. Your author friend will be thrilled beyond words—and that in itself is an incredible feat.

> *Denmark*: When a couple celebrates their silver anniversary, a gate of honor is built from pine branches in front of their home.

Anniversary Bashes

Wedding anniversaries are a private time for a couple to remember years spent together and to anticipate greater days to come.

For our fifth anniversary, I resorted to the traditional suggestion on the gift list: wood. I had my shopping cut out for me, but finally found my answer in an import shop in Corona del Mar, California—a huge, hand-carved wooden chair, which once sat on the wide porch of a British home in India.

Be creative and think outside the anniversary-list constraints. Interpret the recommendations any way you want. On your thirty-fifth, you and your beau may decide it is time to learn to dive for pearls. Maybe you will be the lucky one.

Retro Parties

If throwing a party for the special couple celebrating their twenty-fifth or fiftieth wedding anniversary, why not recreate the past? With a little thought, research, and extra hands, prepare food popular decades ago and play radio hits from their first decade together. On the invitation, encourage the guests to dress in the fashionable styles of yesteryear, but have a wardrobe of accessories ready for those who arrive out of costume.

At this celebration, present an anniversary album to the happy couple. Prior to party time, fill the pages with headlines from today's newspaper, current music, information about the popular food and cars of the moment, and clothing trends. Also include a copy of the invitation, a list of those invited, and other tidbits all about them.

With a Polaroid camera, let various guests play photographer in order to fill the pages as the evening progresses. Ask the guests to write a memory of the wedding (if they attended) and the reason why they believe this happy couple has stayed married all these years. In addition to providing wonderful new memories, this anniversary gala will bring back those from many years ago.

Borrow this "Go Retro" party idea for birthdays, high school or college reunions, or retirement parties, too. Remember anything goes—it is a party! Have fun!

Gone, But Not Forgotten

In the celebration of life, we also must learn new ways to accept death. Americans need to create a positive tradition in recognition of those who may have passed on, but still bring brightness to the lives of those they touched while here on earth.

There will be no question about what I want upon my leaving. My family and friends will have an itinerary of fun activities, a list of my favorite foods, and instructions to play only the best music from all of my decades—loudly and throughout the day and night.

In Mexico, *el Día de los Muertos*, or the Day of the Dead, is celebrated on November 2 and is a day designated to celebrate the past lives of the departed. Families take time to visit the cemetery and place flowers around the

> On November 2, many cultures celebrate those who have passed on with a tribute to All Soul's Day.

graves of their loved ones who have passed away. Music and food abound at this celebration of life and death.

Irish wakes are notorious for all-night drinking, singing, dancing, storytelling, and other amusements. The custom was originally meant to honor the recently deceased with a feast. In the lyrics of many Irish folk songs, the main purpose of these lively bashes was to confirm that the dearly departed was indeed dead. If the dancing, loud music, and laughter did not wake him up...well, so be it. As these affairs degenerated into merrymaking, and the revelry and drunkenness became a scandal with the advent of the Reformation, wakes as feasts and parties became obsolete in England. Instead, an all-night service of prayer and meditation kept vigil in commemoration of the dead.

Once again, until we discover our own way, I suggest adopting another culture's tradition—with your own spin, of course. In your first annual celebration of the Day of the Dead, bring together a group of your closest friends who can each in their own way note the passing of a loved one.

Ask each guest to bring items that the deceased enjoyed and build a shrine in their honor. This celebration of a full life should be positive and light. The loved ones who have passed away would not want it any other way. At nightfall, proceed to the local cemetery. Recognize others who have lived in this place and time and made a difference in our world by burning a small candle on their headstones.

You may choose to celebrate a funeral in a new way with the renaming of this life milestone, perhaps calling it a memorial or a wake and making it a tribute to all that this person has done and who they have touched.

Snapshots of Life for the Graduate

If you have a high-school or college graduate in the house, make an album of his first eighteen years. Start the trip down memory lane with baby pictures, elementary report cards, precious artwork, and toothless school pictures. Along with snapshots from

> You are educated. Your certification is in your degree. You may think of it as the ticket to the good life. Let me ask you to think of an alternative. Think of it as your ticket to change the world.
> —*Tom Brokaw (b. 1940)*

> A graduation ceremony is an event where the commencement speaker tells thousands of students dressed in identical caps and gowns that "individuality" is the key to success.
> —*Robert Orben (b. 1927)*

birthday parties, holidays, and good times with friends, include a "proud" letter from Mom and Dad. At the back of the album, add letters and notes that friends and family have written about the graduate, their earlier memories of the younger student, and any worldly advice for the future.

Tuck inspirational quotes (your own and borrowed) around the margins of every page to give the young adult permission to not only dream, but also live his dream.

Surprise the graduate with tickets to a theme park for her and her friends.

Retirement: A New Lease on Life

Retirement is a huge life change, and for many it can be rather a shock. This individual goes from being in demand and on center stage to a life of few or no demands. Life changes suddenly, and even though it is well deserved and welcomed, it can be a difficult transition. For some, it takes a long time to do because they have been at work for so many years. It is what they know and it is what is comfortable (most of the time).

Help this person with supportive words as soon as she voices her decision.

When she first talks of retirement, send a "You deserve it" card via snail mail or email. Once officially announced, make a congratulatory phone call. At her retirement party, a personal appearance with your good wishes will be appreciated, but if you cannot attend, send a care package to help with the transition into her new life. Help to open this special person's eyes and ears to the possibilities on the other side of life.

This new freedom allows them the time to do whatever might have been put aside earlier in life. But first they probably just want to relax and put their feet up all day long on the very first Monday, Tuesday, and Wednesday that they do not have to report to work.

Surprise the retiree with treats to ease into this quiet, peaceful time: new slippers, a subscription to a hobby magazine, an inspirational calendar or book of quotes, a journal to capture all of her plans for the future, sparkling mineral water from Italy with a decorative bottle ideal for just sitting around, or if you have come into some money, a gift certificate for a massage or facial, or a trial membership at the health club or yoga studio.

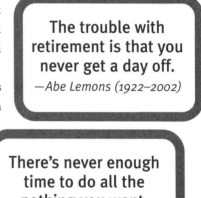

> **The trouble with retirement is that you never get a day off.**
> —*Abe Lemons (1922–2002)*

> **There's never enough time to do all the nothing you want.**
> —*Bill Watterson (b. 1958)*

Surprise her with tickets to an upcoming musical.

What has she always dreamed of but was too busy to pursue earlier in life? Provide the tools and motivation; help her to remember with a special care package designed by you.

Gift-giving Ideas

As we move through this life, we manage to accumulate much baggage. How much more stuff can our closets, attics, basements, and (unfortunately) storage units hold? There is also the cost of gifts to consider, plus the distance between friends and family that makes

> **Half of our life is spent trying to find something to do with the time we have rushed through life trying to save.**
> —*Will Rogers (1879–1935)*

> **It is the mark of an educated mind to be able to entertain a thought without accepting it.**
> —*Aristotle (384–322 BC)*

it increasingly difficult to figure out what exactly this person could use or even want.

Money and gift certificates work for some celebrations, but most of the time, we would like to give something that truly matters.

Why not give from the heart?

If your artistic talents are developed, draw a picture, frame it, and wrap it for the lucky recipient. Proficient with a camera—disposable, digital, or 35 mm—shoot it and send it to someone who means the world to you.

Handmade items also send a greater message of "I care." Know how to make soap, scented candles, paper and stationery, dried floral wreaths, or infused herbal oils? If you are so blessed in this regard, share.

Is writing your secret love? Draft a memory book for Dad on Father's Day. Simply begin each sentence with: *"I remember…"* and see what happens. Find photos of both of you from long ago; either include them with your words or make copies of the cherished photos as the opening page to each section.

Memory Book: At the retirement party at work, create a photo album just for the woman of the hour. Fill this memory book with photos to cover the span of her diligent career. Tag the photos with humorous captions or cartoon thought bubbles written by you and fellow associates.

Don't have Dad's memory book done for mailing in June? Keep writing—the holidays are still six months away. Missed that date, too? Shoot for his birthday again.

Feel free to borrow this idea for Mother's Day, graduations, anniversaries, retirement, and birthdays, too.

Can you bake? Whip up one of your all-time favorite recipes and package it the way Martha Stewart would—pretty box, bow, and handmade card. Be sure to include the ingredient list (in case of food allergies) and baking instructions if she loves it.

Can you sew, quilt, knit, or crochet? Something made by hand will be treasured for generations and much appreciated in this disposable world.

If you are a poet, pen several poems about this person. I bet it could be the

> If you choose to give a gift certificate, provide a small token to hint at the gift that you are suggesting. For example, if you give a certificate to a bookstore, add a bookmark and perhaps a list of influential books that you have enjoyed.

> If you choose to give money as a gift, why not try a memorable presentation of two-dollar bills, silver dollars, or stock certificates?

first chapbook that they ever received and definitely the only one written about them. Create a decorative cover for your book of poetry, including a dedication page and a title page with your byline, date of publication, and a list of the poem titles. What a wonderful anniversary present to your partner, son or daughter, grandparents, or anyone else dear to you.

Prefer talking to writing? Why not send a talking book instead about this person to honor his birthday or other special occasion? Record your thoughts, memories, or advice on an audiocassette, MP3 clip, or CD for your coworker leaving the workplace, your child headed off to college, or your newborn baby.

If you are musically inclined, record yourself singing your favorite song or music written by you—and send it. What a magnificent gift to be able to sing or play music; please share your talents.

Like to be in front of the camera? Can you dance or tell jokes? Create a video in honor of this special person and ship it with a bag of popcorn and a homemade movie ticket warning the viewer of the content of the video.

Do you tell great stories? Send a video tale to your brother's or sister's kids telling them all about their dad or mom when they were just little kids. (I need to do this for my brother's boys next Christmas—the stories I could tell them...)

> **If you can walk, you can dance; if you can talk, you can sing!**
> —*Zimbabwe proverb*

Love Books? Buy a small journal and fill it up with words, pictures, poetry, and compliments for Mom. She will treasure it always. Grandmas, grandpas, dads, brothers, and sisters will also be appreciative of this gift from the heart—from yours to theirs.

Coupon Booklets

These homemade tokens of favors and special treatments will give you "angel status" here on earth. Use whatever you have to make these coupon booklets, or buy one appropriate for your sentiments. With paper, colored pens, computer clip-art, and a stapler, your books of fun, love, and appreciation are done easily. Remember, since it bears repeating, it is the thought that counts. Here are several suggestions to get started:

- Ink your foot and stamp your footprint on several pieces of paper to create foot-massage coupons. Punch a hole in one toe and tie them all together. Add the message *Good for a free massage anytime.*
- For hand-massage coupons, cut out shapes of your hand and connect them at the wrist.

- Make coupons out of paper plates with the words *No Dishes on Monday* written on each one.
- Copy recipes and add the words *Will Cook Dinner on Thursday* across the top.
- Attach a note to a few dry sheets that reads *Will Fold Laundry Anytime.*

Date Nights: On anniversaries, spouses can earn extra brownie points with a coupon booklet of proposed date nights with a time and date already inked for a whole year of togetherness.

Family Fun Nights

Coupon booklets filled with ideas for a Family Fun Night are a good tool to get everyone helping around the house. Go through the phone book and copy the ads of the family's favorite spots to frequent: batting cage, ice-skating rink, driving range, miniature golf, the local pizzeria, movie theater, and sundae shop. Flip to the front of the phone book and be sure to add the no-cost coupons in nature, too: parks, rivers, lakes, libraries, and free days at the museums.

After the work is done around the house or yard, let one of the little ones pick a coupon to cash in that night or over the weekend.

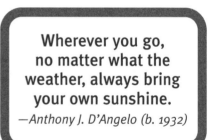

Wherever you go, no matter what the weather, always bring your own sunshine.
—*Anthony J. D'Angelo (b. 1932)*

Timeless Gifts

When we pass through moments in our lives, be it the big 5-0, the arrival of a new baby, or a graduation, we want to mark this day in a way different from all the other celebrations over the decades. To do something that will be remembered and cherished, I believe in giving gifts that also grow with time. Here are few ideas of timeless gifts:

- Plant a tree when a child is born.
- Buy two U.S. Saving Bonds when a young couple marries.

- Have a star named for a graduate.
- Order a vanity license plate to acknowledge the new driver in the household.
- Buy stocks for a new adult on her 21st birthday.
- Take an eighteen-year-old who is going to vote for the first time to Washington, D.C.
- For a young adult's 21st birthday, have a professional portrait painted or photographed.
- Order the family's crest or coat of arms for a retirement gift.
- Trace the family tree and present the findings for a silver-anniversary present.
- Take a graduate to have her stars or horoscope read.

> Everything ends this way in France—everything. Weddings, christenings, duels, burials, swindlings, diplomatic affairs—everything is a pretext for a good dinner.
> —Jean Anouilh (1910–1987)

chapter 6

great
TRADITIONS

*making memories

> **Spring is when you feel like whistling even with a shoe full of slush.**
> —*Doug Larson (1902–1981)*

Why simply celebrate what the calendar dictates year after year? Start your own traditions. Your new holiday could be based on a national, agricultural, or religious event, or something that you dream up all on your own, something that you feel strongly about, or something that you want to recognize in a grand way.

Springtime Traditions
Helping Hands

Together with your family, plant a vegetable garden—even the littlest of hands can help dig the small holes for the seeds or water the garden with a spray bottle.

Want to get to know the neighbors better? Why not broach the subject of creating a cooperative garden patch and work together to reap the harvest.

If your patio-sized yard does not permit the magnitude that you envision for your bounty of fresh vegetables and

Need to learn new ways to cook more often with vegetables? Mark your calendar for the annual Vegetarian Summerfest, sponsored by the North American Vegetarian Society (518) 568-7970.

flowers, perhaps you can address the matter with the landlord or homeowner's association board and get permission to create a garden for all in one of the common green areas.

Queen-for-the-Day

This is the crown jewel of all gifts—ideal for any woman from 8 to 108. Use this "Queen-for-the-Day" idea to celebrate birthdays, high-school or college graduations, the bride-to-be, expectant mothers, Mother's Day, retirement, or any unofficial day to make a woman or girl feel like royalty.

Mother's Day has been celebrated in the United States since 1908. The sons and daughters of Australia, Denmark, Finland, Turkey, and Canada also pay tribute to their mothers on this special day. France's version of Mother's Day, *Fête de Mères*, is celebrated on the last Sunday in May, and the good citizens of the United Kingdom call the last Sunday of March "Mothering Sunday." Norwegians and Argentineans toast their moms on the second Sunday of February, while the Spanish and Portuguese wait to celebrate their mothers on December 8.

Shower her with love, attention, and the respect reserved for those with a royal bloodline. My suggestion is to fill a large box—perhaps a hat box or decorative storage box—with a regal robe, fancy beaded slippers, a small box of chocolates, a bottle of perfume or scented lotion, a paper Japanese fan, a dinner bell to ring for service, a "Do Not Disturb" door sign, and on top of the wondrous pile—a rhinestone tiara.

Inside the crown, tuck a scroll of the responsibilities that she will *not* do on this particular day. Be sure to have a camera ready for her big smile of gratitude. She will never forget this day.

Summertime Traditions

Make it a Saturday morning ritual to visit the local farmer's market with your spouse, son, or daughter. Not only will you support the local economy, but you'll also teach your children a healthy way to eat. When they watch you adopt this holistic approach to living—using fresh fruits, vegetables, and herbs in your cooking as often as you can, your actions will speak louder than words.

Arbor Day

In 1872, the first Arbor Day took place in June and was considered a great success, with more than one million trees planted. Julius Sterling Morton, credited with the idea, believed that planting trees would not only provide beauty and timber, but also serve as a windbreak and help hold the soil on the Nebraska plains. Fortunately, other countries besides the United States—Bolivia, Canada, Korea, Lesotho, and Soviet Union—continue to back his conviction about preservation.

In addition to planting trees on Arbor Day, why not elaborate on this idea and initiate a clean-up day for your neighborhood? Author Malcolm Gladwell of *The Tipping Point: How Little Things Can Make a Big Difference* made a curious yet poignant observation about trash and pride. His research showed that when some people start to litter, others follow. Contrarily, if people take pride in their neighborhood and pick up all trash, fix broken fences and windows, and apply a fresh coat of paint, others follow their lead. Instill your neighborhood with fierce pride. Join families and join forces.

Father's Day

Sonora Louise Smart Dodd of Spokane, Washington, first proclaimed the idea of Father's Day as a tribute to her own father. After his wife died in childbirth, he raised six children as a single parent. In 1924, President Calvin Coolidge endorsed her idea, but it was not until 1966 that President Lyndon Johnson finally signed a proclamation declaring the third Sunday of June to be Father's Day.

> **One father is more than a hundred schoolmasters.**
> —*English proverb*

This Father's Day, kindly ask Dad to step aside from his grilling area. It is your turn to show him your surprises from the grill. Also take over any household task that Dad would just love to have taken off his "to do" list.

Canada and England also pay homage to fathers on this special day. In Australia and France, Father's Day is celebrated on the first Sunday of September, while in Brazil, Dad is recognized on the second Sunday of August and in Spain, on March 19.

> **It is a wise father that knows his own child.**
> —*William Shakespeare (c. 1564–1616)*

Patriotic Traditions

This Fourth of July holiday, *participate* in something amusing rather than simply watching fireworks. Enter a float or start your own neighborhood parade. Invite the tykes to decorate their tricycles, doll carriages, or wagons. Give new parents red, white, and blue streamers and balloons to decorate their baby strollers. If you can, rope off the street for your first annual parade and block party.

Part of the formula for any successful outing is to involve as many as possible to make each person feel part of the group. Get the kids in on the celebration, too, and ask them to deliver block party reminder flyers one week before the event.

Give the judges paper plates and magic markers to have them rate the contestants as they pass on a scale of one to ten. Tell them that they are only permitted to give out 9.5, 9.9, and perfect scores of 10. Put out a fish bowl with slips of paper and pencils to allow everyone to vote for the most creative costume, the brightest entry, the most patriotic, and the funniest. Award the winners red, white, or blue ribbons, and give lollipops of the same colors to all participants.

On the Fourth of July and for Thanksgiving, be patriotic and support your local wineries—serve only American wines.

Pennsylvania: Lititz Springs Park begins its patriotic festivities with the lighting of more than seven thousand candles prior the fireworks show.

Make sure you assign someone the job of photographer. If she's using a digital camera, give her assistant a pad of paper to take down emails in order to send the winning smiles home later that week.

Put a few of the older kids in charge of the evening's nighttime show. Tell them that you will provide the lightning (flashlights), props (a box of dress-up clothes), and the AV system (a boom box). Set up the seating area for the adults and the younger children. All that is required is your attention and loud applause.

Recognition and appreciation go a long way, too. Be sure to announce the names of all of those who help make this fun party possible. Use the karaoke machine to make sure that your "Thanks!" are heard.

Afterward, pass out glow sticks for a safe and fun alternative to fireworks. Tie the various available colors to kite string and let the kids run wild with a trail of gleaming light following them. Their restless energy will add brilliant streaks of color to the warm evening.

USA Road Trips

A long weekend of patriotic celebration is the perfect opportunity to witness how other Americans honor this 225-plus-year-old tradition. Why not take to the open roads and see for yourself? North on California's route 395 is a beautiful drive, past the tallest mountain in North America, Mount Whitney, to Mammoth Lakes, California, nestled at seventy-eight hundred feet above sea level.

Rhode Island: This year, take a road trip to Bristol and be front and center at the oldest Fourth of July parade in the country.

This little mountain town, still filled with ample piles of snow in July, makes their annual parade a hoot. Be ready to participate because this is where the fire department and other citizens on feisty floats get in the spirit of having snowball battles with the crowds lining the streets. The spectators and participants are not below resorting to water guns and water balloons either. Watch out, though; the fire department has mighty hoses, which can—without a doubt—reach their target.

La Torta dei Fieschi

Talk about memorable weddings. In 1240, Count Fieschi of Lavagna in Genoa amazed his guests when he presented a wedding cake more than ten yards high. He shared slices with all of his guests as well as the townfolks.

Today, Genoa still celebrates "Fieschi's Cake." At nightfall, women and men dressed in period costumes write a word on a slip of paper and search the crowd for someone who has written the same word on his or her piece of paper. These couples are awarded a piece of cake.

Try this "word-search game" at your next party. My suggestion is to use racy Italian words or expressions. Consult your local Italian dictionary and have a delicious *tiramisu* waiting for the lucky couples.

Autumn-time Traditions
Cherishing Grandparents

Celebrate Grandparent's Day on the first Sunday of September. Spend time with them if you are close by, listen to their stories, record what they have to say with pen and paper, video, or audiocassette. We need to know our past and those close to us, and they need reasons to celebrate the older years of their lives. In doing so, we get a glimpse of history, which we will never see if we do not ask. We need to know their stories. These people in our lives are much wiser than we are. Listen and learn.

> **Autumn is a second spring when every leaf is a flower.**
> —*Albert Camus (1913–1960)*

Pffiferdaj

In France on the "Day of the Flutes," the city of Ribeauvillé celebrates its unique musical history. In tribute to the Ribeaupierre family, who started a powerful musician's union in Alsace during the Middle Ages, and to honor the church of Our Lady of Dusenbach, their patron, a procession of musicians gather at the foot of the Vosges Mountains every September. Jugglers, troubadours, and minstrels join this parade of musicians who play old-world instruments, meandering through town and past the main square's fountain, which supposedly flows with wine.

Whether you begin your own musical tribute to your favorite musicians in your own backyard or jaunt across the world to experience other traditions, start this year. You will be glad you welcomed music and its party into your life. If your children play, honor their talents, and let them put on private concerts for you as often as they would like. Wouldn't you be proud to be sitting in Carnegie Hall fifteen years from now watching your child perform?

Vacation Traditions

During my childhood, my family took frequent trips to Cape Cod, Massachusetts, requiring very long car rides from Pennsylvania. My most vivid memories of these trips—besides my bare legs sticking to the vinyl of our '73 Impala—were the cranberry bogs and the countless ways the locals served the red berries.

I remember the intriguing sight of hundreds of thousands of those red berries bobbing on the top of the flooded bogs. I had a hard time being convinced by my parents that the farmers actually flooded a perfectly good field in order to harvest the berries. I did not believe them until I saw it done.

Cranberries, which contain the compound ellagic acid, are a great way to block the effects of damaging free radicals, and drinking cranberry juice helps to maintain urinary tract health.

I remember the warm thick slices of cranberry bread, the top-heavy cranberry muffins, and the small glasses of the ruby-colored, tart juice served with a wedge of lemon at almost every one of our meals. Now, every time I bake any cranberry treat for my family, I can still taste the warmth of those vacations from thirty years ago.

Massachusetts: Since 1949, the largest cranberry festival is held every autumn in South Carver.

The best time to visit Massachusetts is when the cranberry bogs are harvested in late September or early October. The Cape Cod bike trail, built on the tracks of former railroads, will take you past the small ponds teeming with floating red berries. Two-thirds of all the cranberries in the United States are grown here in this little state. Americans eat about 117 million pounds of cranberries a year, most of it during November and December—but you do not have to abstain until the holidays.

Cranberry cocktail juice sold in grocery stores is processed and loaded with sugar. Choose the unsweetened version, but if you find it too tart, mix with pure apple juice.

*

Blueberry Festivals:
May: Alma, Georgia (912) 632-5859
June: Brewton, Alabama (215) 867-3224
August: Machias, Maine (207) 255-6665
August: Frankfort, Michigan (989) 845-2080

Find a fruit and head off on an adventure in its honor. Who knows where this exploration will take you and how often—perhaps it will become a regular family tradition.

There are many reasons to head out on a worthwhile excursion, be it in the name of starting a new family tradition of picking fresh berries, tasting treasures created around a sole ingredient such as the intoxicating smell of garlic, or bounties of just harvested seafood—whatever your pleasure. Make your outing a field day or an extended road trip and let your vacation evolve around food and the celebration of good living. During the exploration of your new tradition, remember to play and nap—playing makes for a hearty appetite, and napping provides the rested mind you need to appreciate the good food and good times.

Baking Traditions

Ovens only became a fixture in Italian households after World War II and are still used today by many to dry and store homemade cheeses. Prior to their arrival in the kitchen, the village communal oven or the local baker would bake your lasagna or bread.

Turn this appliance in your kitchen into another reason to gather around with your children or grandchildren, your spouse or good friends, and start the tradition of making bread, pies, scones, tarts, tortes, or whatever moves you to try to bake. Mothers, teach your sons to make a peach pie and make your future daughter-in-law your biggest fan.

On a rainy day, decide that the whole group will learn how to make ravioli, gnocchi, or *baklava*. Set a date with your grandmother or grandfather to get insider information. Let this afternoon be one of togetherness and an opportunity to hear history firsthand. If Grandma lives too far away, check out a cookbook from the library or invite over a talented friend to learn how to make tamales, wontons, or half-moon pies.

American Pie

My sister-in-law Laura stepped in and assisted my daughter with the fine points of baking. She taught her how to make an apple pie from scratch—including the pie dough. Brittany's first pie was excellent and her confidence was so great that by the time Thanksgiving rolled around, my ten-year-old insisted on making the annual feast's apple pie.

I like these aunt-and-niece traditions. I hope the learning continues; Laura also makes an excellent cheesecake!

Wintertime Traditions

In Southern Italy, the locals welcome in the New Year in a rather peculiar, yet festive manner. At midnight on New Year's Eve, it is customary to hurl old pots, tarnished pans, and even old worn furniture out the window. This literal translation of the expression "Out with the old and in with the new" may be a new tradition to start, but you might want to warn the neighbors first.

This holiday season, why not start your own tradition of planting your Christmas tree after enjoying it inside? Check with your local nursery in early November to ensure that there will be a tree ready for your new custom.

Many Americans make it a tradition to attend the Rose Parade held in Pasadena, California, every year on New Year's Day. Started in 1890, the parade resembles the Festival of Flowers held in Nice, France. Word to the wise: tickets go on sale eleven months prior to the parade, so reserve your grandstand seats now.

Belleville, Pennsylvania: Created by the Amish, half-moon pies are yummy snacks. They are made from a mixture of peeled and sliced apples spiced with cinnamon, sugar, and butter, then spooned onto a circular piece of pastry dough a tad thicker than pie dough, folded in half, sealed, and baked to perfection. This treat is definitely worthy of your search for this Amish recipe or to discover a little hamlet where they are sold.

Before the ground freezes, survey your yard as to where to plant your new addition and dig the hole. Cover the hole with straw. Keep the soil in the heated garage or somewhere else warm for the planting later. Prior to planting the tree outdoors, move it to a cool place for two days to adjust. Remember to water your tree when it is inside and again when planted outside. Every year, add to your forest and make the world a healthier place to live.

Santa Visits

This holiday ritual is easy to start with a visit to the local costume-rental store.

From my earliest memories, a full-size Santa Claus would waltz through our front door unannounced a few evenings before Christmas Eve. My brother, sister, and I would be dumbfounded. This tradition continued for about five years until we moved away. Later I discovered that my father's good friend, Jim Schnell, had played the jolly role.

Merry Traditions

In the sixteenth century, the concept of "toasting" began—a small piece of bread would be placed in a goblet of wine. The guests would take a sip and pass it along until it reached the guest of honor, who then drained the goblet and ate the morsel at the bottom.

Do you know why it is tradition to clink glasses after a toast? Rumor has it that it's to include the fifth sense of hearing. When we hold the fine stemware in hand and admire its color and bouquet before tasting, then clink our glasses, we are experiencing the moment with all of our senses.

The holidays are a time of wishing each other good cheer. If you tire of simply saying, "Cheers!" deviate and throw in a few foreign expressions for good measure and luck:

Danish: *Skaal!*

Armenian: *Genatsoot!* (Life!)

> **"I think this calls for a drink" has long been one of our national slogans.**
> —James Thurber (1894–1961)

Spanish: *Salud!*
French: *À votre santé!* (To your health!)
Hawaiian: *Okole maluna!*
Polish: *Nazdrowie!* (To your health!)

The Kissing Tradition

In England, the Victorian custom of hanging a kissing ball made of evergreens and mistletoe above an interior doorway treated those who paused beneath it to a kiss, bestowed by the owner of the home.

The Welsh say you should kiss beneath the mistletoe at Yuletide to stay in love. Customary beliefs advised unmarried women with the following warning: if you refuse a kiss, even from a stranger, you will remain a spinster your entire life. Further, if you sleep with mistletoe under your pillow, you will dream of the man you will marry.

Nonalcoholic Beverage Alternatives:
- Sparkling apple cider served in champagne flutes
- Tonic and lime on the rocks
- Virgin piña coladas garnished with a pineapple spear, then topped with a cherry and paper drink umbrella
- Virgin margaritas rimmed in salt (or sugar if serving the strawberry version)
- Virgin Bloody Marys—the extra spicy version—with a flamboyant stalk of celery and three green olives speared on a plastic sword or bamboo skewer
- Nonalcoholic beer served in a frosted mug
- Nonalcoholic wine in a red wine goblet or a white wine glass

Mistletoe, growing wild in the trees of Calaveras County, where my husband grew up and his parents still have Long's Christmas Tree Farm, is considered a nuisance because of its parasitic nature. Every holiday, we would pick fresh bunches of mistletoe from the grateful trees to give to friends in Southern California for the purpose of kissing often. Why not see if your local Christmas tree farm would benefit from some mistletoe seekers? You can harvest your own while picking out your tree every year.

The Essence of Time

Martha Stewart has wonderful ideas and suggestions to spruce up any celebration; however, most of us do not have a staff of forty to help us, and consider our nightly sleep a mandatory factor in our continued pursuit of happiness. I vote to remove some of the rushed feeling around the holidays and other obligatory occasions to celebrate.

Instead of giving "more stuff" for holidays, birthdays, or a retirement party, come up with your own ideas to reinforce the significance of the wise old adage "It is the thought that counts." Place your emphasis on the creativity behind gift giving. Cleverness or thoughtfulness—not the price—counts with your new, innovative gift ideas.

To replace the rush felt at the holidays with peacefulness and thankfulness, borrow a few of these ideas:

1. Give IOUs. Make the note grand, and place it in a box with confetti, telling the recipient that a secret gift will be delivered on a certain date or to reserve a date for a special outing. Give the gift of time—it is the most valuable present you can give.
2. Host an open-house party later in January to wish friends and neighbors a happy New Year.
3. Choose to celebrate your new traditions in a slower month—March, August, or September.
4. Keep a list of birthdays and anniversaries and other important dates and events to remember in your bag. When you are at an incredible sale, peruse your list and find the right gift for the right person—and on sale.
5. Buy gift wrap after the holidays and store it away for next year.
6. Pick up birthday and anniversary cards months ahead of time. It will be less stressful and rewarding to have your own Hallmark store conveniently at home. Don't forget to stock stamps, too.

Traditional Memories

Instead of writing the annual Christmas letter telling everyone of your accomplishments of the year, why not write a few key letters to those whose presence in your life you really appreciate?

Have you ever thanked your parents? In writing? Tell them of all the wonderful things that they have done for you.

Have you ever told your siblings some of the great memories that you have from your childhood? Retell them the stories that they told you, but tell them from your perspective. Letters from the heart like these will be cherished. Your letter could be told in captions under old photos in an album, a series of twelve postcards symbolizing the twelve days of Christmas, or written on a long roll of butcher paper with illustrations that further reveal the story in a cartoon fashion.

What are you waiting for? The holidays will be here before you know it. Start your Christmas in July. You might want to bake some cookies and put on seasonal music to get you in the mood.

Special Delivery

Care packages are just what they say—you care enough to spend time thinking of the person and packing trinkets to send them.

Within days after I arrived home from the hospital with my brand new baby daughter, my husband opened the door to Lois, the lady from whom I rented office space and who had become a good friend, too. She hauled in a large cooler filled with homemade and easy-to-heat-up dinners, oatmeal cookies, and other treats. I was flabbergasted. My husband was hungry just at the sight of all the wonderful dishes that she had taken the time to make and deliver.

My good friend Tom's mom had another twist on "care packages." While he was away at college, every year for his birthday she would bake a cake, ice it, and ship it to him in a box. You can only imagine the condition of his birthday cake, but with a houseful of collegiate male track runners, it was devoured and enjoyed no matter what it looked like.

My mother perfected this type of anticipation and surprise. Scavenger and treasure hunts, doll shows, parades, haunted houses, ghost stories, care packages—she gave from the heart and usually on a zero budget. Whenever I made any step toward adulthood, my mother always packed a care package to make the transition a bit easier. Off to tennis camp, college, or a move across the country from my little town in Pennsylvania, the brown-paper-wrapped box always showed up a few days after I did or was packed among my clothes. What a treat. (What a mom.)

Below are also some very good reasons to deliver a care package to those who will truly appreciate the gesture:

> Make even the most ordinary meal—lunch—a care package, too, even if you just add a sweet note.

Off to College

Pack comfort items to make a squished dorm room a home: new bedding, lounging pillows, picture frames, corkboard and push pins, snacks, mad money for pizza, and a phone card. After the first semester, send a stationery package complete with personalized return mailing labels, a box of cards, a new pen and address book, plus stamps. Inquire if you can order these labels from the college print shop with the university's crest and logo on them to acknowledge the new adult in the family.

Anniversaries

Create a care package to celebrate your wedding with your significant other. Fill a fancy box with a postcard from your honeymoon, a copy of the wedding program, snapshots from the reception, the guest book and wedding album, a bathrobe or another item from the gift shop at the hotel where you stayed, or perhaps a gift representative of the area that you first toured as husband and wife. Also include a dual photo frame of the couple you both became on that special day, and then add a new picture of the couple that you are today.

New Life

Help a family member, friend, or business associate adjust to a new job relocation or move into a different career with a care package. Letters and cards will work well to carry your good wishes, but sometimes the unexpected will do wonders. Consider what they may need. If it is their very first house, the basics might be welcomed: a hammer and picture-hanging kit with various hooks and wire, paper towels with window and counter cleaner, can opener, bottle opener, snacks, drinks, room spray or a scented candle, enchanting music like *Gypsy Caravan* or an energizing option such as the Fleetwood Mac CD *Say You Will* to get a tired body to unpack just one more box.

If the move is to a new job, you might want to help make the desk or office more comfortable: an attractive vase for future flowers (be sure to send her favorite the first week of work); an aromatherapy ceramic diffuser with an illuminating essential oil to try, such as clary sage; a fancy pen to inspire her to be creative and productive; a water carafe with matching glass for her desktop; a whimsical mouse pad to make her smile; and perhaps a wall or desk calendar filled with inspirational quotes or soothing images.

New Baby Arrival

A coupon book filled with offers to baby-sit, run errands, cook dinner, or help out around the house are better than any baby-shower gift.

Travel Care Package

Surprise your friend or boss on her next business or pleasure trip with small revival kit. Include: a small package of tea bags along with a few packets of raw sugar tied with a ribbon, a small tube of scented hand lotion preferably created with essential oil of lavender or eucalyptus, peppermint candies to soothe an upset stomach, a travel aromatherapy candle, and a tiny book of inspirational quotes. Wrap it all up in a scarf with a handwritten *bon voyage* note.

Other presents could include: a travel-sized sound machine with an alarm, a portable CD player with headset and a CD, or an herbal eye pillow.

Hocus Pocus on the Road

Since a long road trip for children is anything over an hour, start the tradition of "Hocus Pocus." We created this ritual with a story we

Happy Toes: Know a good friend who is always on the go? Inspire her to kick off her high heels anytime. Pamper her weary feet with a little goody bag. Include a couple of small bottles of nail polish, a tube of soothing lotion, and new pair of flip-flops. If it is wintertime, substitute a pair of slipper socks for the inexpensive sandals. Either way, she will be thrilled and so will her toes.

repeatedly told our daughter. Once the car hits a certain speed, enough magic is generated inside to instantly produce wrapped gifts. With closed eyes and little hands outstretched, she had to say "hocus pocus" three times.

This stall would give me enough time to wrestle a small gift from under the passenger seat. From coloring book and crayons to scented magic markers, stickers and books, packs of gum, mints, or even a candy bar, chapstick, lotion, and later lipstick, crossword puzzle and word-search books, novels, and battery-operated and hand-held sports and video games, the car looked like Christmas morning when we finally arrived. This little game made for hours of peace within our small confined area.

Two notes of caution: save about one-third of the prizes for the ride home, and do not forget the other adult in the car. A wrapped magazine, a snack, a new book on tape, CD, or book will bring a wide smile from your appreciative passenger.

The price point of these gifts is irrelevant. It is, again, the thought that counts. Choose a horoscope or crossword puzzle booklet found at the grocery checkout stand, or check the aisle of the birthday-party prizes. Be creative in your selection, and make sure the gift will provide an hour or more of fun or is interactive, something that everyone in the car can play.

To cut costs, I often wrap the gifts in the bags that they come in and tie them up with lots of curling ribbon to increase the anticipation or use the Sunday comics for cheap, but colorful wrap. We often read the comics aloud to pass the time, too.

Welcome to the Neighborhood

The customary and yet always appreciated gift is a plate of homemade cookies or other snack to keep the unpacking energy level high.

Quick dinners such as hearty soups or Texan-style spicy chili delivered with a loaf of bread will also be welcomed. If your culinary skills are on the same level as mine or time does not permit you to make two dinners, stop by the grocery store, pick up a small cooler, and load it up with beverages and ice.

Birthday Traditions

To celebrate your birthday in a truly new fashion, adopt any of these international traditions or make up your own:

- Buy a special birthday plate for the birthday honoree's meals.
- Implement the new birthday rule that in order to open your presents, the birthday guy must run around the block as many times as years he has lived.
- Tie a red ribbon to the foot of the sleeping child's bed. In the morning, she follows the ribbon to her special stash of birthday presents.

Kidnap Birthday Breakfasts: Awaken the birthday girl and carry her in her pajamas with pillow and blanket to the decorated car. Circulate among her friends' houses and repeat the kidnapping procedure. Celebrate at her favorite breakfast restaurant. Don't forget the bouquet of balloons to tie to her chair.

International Birthday Traditions:

Argentina and Brazil: The birthday child gets her earlobe pulled for as many years as she has been alive.

China: Money is the common gift given at the traditional noodle lunch where family and friends are invited. Symbolism influences much of Chinese life, and food is no exception. Noodles are served at this special time because of the belief that eating them will ensure the gift of longevity.

Germany: At sunrise, mom awakens and lights the number of candles corresponding to the birthday person's years, plus one for good luck. The candles are left burning all day. In the evening, there is a birthday party with the traditional song (sung in German) while the birthday girl blows out all the candles in one mighty swift breath to make wishes come true.

India: At school the birthday child wears a colored dress and with the help of a friend, passes out chocolates to the entire class.

Ireland: The birthday child is picked up and "bumped" on the floor for each year and an extra one for good luck.

Russia: Many Russian children receive a birthday pie with a greeting carved into its crust.

- Buy your children a book each year.
- Celebrate half-birthdays. Everything is done in half on the six-month date. Half a cake, cups half full, only the first two lines of "Happy Birthday," and a gift of half of something. This practice may make the approaching birthday, at least for some adults, not such a shock.

Birthdays are a wonderful time to tell a friend or business associate whose advice you appreciate how much you enjoy her being in your life. Besides the traditional answers for a gift, why not give a potted plant of her birth month's flower?

With a little water and sunshine, this present will last as long as your friendship. However, if this special person is known to be a black thumb, you might want to offer a bouquet of the cherished flower instead. If she is a renowned gardener, perhaps a packet of seeds with the offer to help plant them might be more meaningful.

Guaranteed Smiles:
- January: **Carnation**
- February: **Violet**
- March: **Jonquil**
- April: **Sweet Pea**
- May: **Lily of the Valley**
- June: **Rose**
- July: **Larkspur**
- August: **Gladiolus**
- September: **Aster**
- October: **Calendula**
- November: **Chrysanthemum**
- December: **Narcissus**

chapter 7

up and AWAY

*picnics and tailgating parties

> Rest is not idleness, and to lie sometime
> on the grass under trees on a summer's day,
> listening to the murmur of the water,
> or watching the clouds float across the sky,
> is by no means a waste of time.
>
> —Sir J. Lubbock (1834–1913)

Life is a picnic and each meal an opportunity to celebrate life wholeheartedly. The choices for your picnics are indeed endless. From Christmas tree–cutting excursions, lunch on a boat, or brunch in the park to tailgating parties, backwoods hikes with gourmet sandwiches packed on your backs, or a romantic portable banquet for two, there are many opportunities to pull the picnic basket together. Experiment with your definition of a picnic—then test it this weekend.

A Picnic by Any Other Name

Prior to the Industrial Age, when men worked in the fields from sunrise to sundown, the woman of the house oftentimes planned an open-air picnic. A feast was served, complete with sliced cold ham, homemade bread served with apple butter, farm fresh cheese, shoofly pie, ginger cakes, fruit from the orchards, and gallons of mint tea—all presented under the comfort of a generous shade tree.

Why not recreate this idyllic setting and place yourself and your family smack dab in the middle of it? Your menu does not have to be grand or all homemade to be called a picnic. Take shortcuts: stop by the deli and pick up two different twelve-inch submarine sandwiches or order a pizza (or two) plus a salad. If it is served outdoors to those sitting on a blanket, it qualifies as a picnic—but even this is not mandatory. A park bench or table will work just as well for a party of five or two.

The Greeks (once again) invented the idea of having a picnic as a communal potluck served in the open air. However, the French named this outdoor repast by combining the root verb *piquer*, to pick, with the nonsensical syllable *nique*.

The Moveable Feast

Leave it to the British to make any dining experience elegant and sometimes extravagant. At their picnics, servants carried the tables, chairs, linens, silver, crystal, china, and bottles of wine. They also packed a hearty picnic basket the size of a steamer trunk with enough food for a week.

> **The more the merrier, the fewer the better fare.**
> —*John Palsgrave (b. ?–1554)*

My advice is to go light with both necessary utensils and food selections. In the middle of a busy week, deliberately take time for a leisurely lunch—it will be like treating yourself to a minivacation. On Sunday night, pack this week's light picnic basket.

Essential Utensils:
- Paper Napkins
- Corkscrew
- Bottle Opener/Knife
- Tablecloth/blanket
- Paper plates
- Cutlery
- Matches and citronella candle
- Salt and pepper
- Glasses/cups
- Hot mitt
- Aluminum foil
- Plastic baggies
- Trash bag
- After-dinner mints

Spring Is Here

Going to a sporting event—your child's, your husband's, yours, or to see a professional team play? Turn mealtime into a tailgating opportunity. Expand the party to include other families and enlist their help. Bring the lawn chairs, a cooler of refreshing drinks, the grill, and the fixings. Select the paper goods in the local team's colors and hang a pennant to show your spirit and support. Set up camp in the parking lot or in the next-door park and enjoy the latter hours of the day without any reason to jump up and go anywhere. Dinner is served. Enjoy the moment.

Al Fresco

Hosting a bridal shower? Make it a garden luncheon. Is it your turn to surprise the mom-to-be with a baby shower? Here is another good excuse for a picnic in the park, lakeside, or at the beach—anywhere outside.

Is there a graduation, a milestone birthday, or retirement party approaching quickly on your calendar? Bring it out of the hotel conference room and breathe the fresh air.

Cater it if you must, but let the group eat, drink, and be merry outdoors. If summer has not quite arrived where you live, set up a tent in case of chancy wet weather. String party lights across the tent's ceiling, among the branches of the trees, or tuck them in the bushes. Light the center of the tables with low candles, so as not to interfere with conversation or eye contact.

This magical night picnic will linger in the guest of honor's memory forever as a special moment.

Make every day a picnic and eat dinner on a blanket. Stake candle holders into the lawn to create a twilight ambiance. If you stay true to the meaning of "Let's have a picnic," clean up will be a breeze. With paper plates, there are no dishes to clean—only more time to relax on a weekday night.

Use any reason to dine *al fresco*. The food will taste better, the conversation will be lively, and peace—for as long as you sit—will be yours.

Spring Picnic Games: Freebie golf—set up your own imaginary course. Try out the Italian version of bowling and hold court on the lawn with a lively game of *bocce*. Keep warm with a fast-moving game of flashlight tag with the kids.

Recycle: Use mason jars with lids to make beverages easier to transport. In a pitcher, mix lemonade with a little less water than required, fill each jar with ice cubes and beverage, and secure the lids tightly. By the time the picnic starts, everyone will have an ice-cold glass of a refreshing beverage—perfect on a scorching summer day.

Avocado Corn Salsa by Bobbie Werk
  2 cups cooked corn
  1 avocado
  1 small can diced green chilies
  ½ cup chopped sweet onion
  ½ cup chopped red bell pepper
  ½ cup chopped mango
  1 tbsp. olive oil
  1 tbsp. red wine vinegar
  1 tbsp. minced garlic
  1½ tsp. ground cumin
  1 tsp. dried oregano
  1 lime

Mash peeled avocado and stir in other ingredients. Add salt and pepper to taste and finish with a generous squeeze of fresh lime. Serve with blue or red corn chips.

A picnic can definitely fit into a weekend day. Try it this weekend: decide to take a stroll in the first hours of dawn. In a backpack or picnic basket, bring along a hot beverage, breakfast pastry, a blanket, and perhaps the newspaper or a good book.

Later in the month, reserve an evening for a sunset hike. Climb to the top of a vista or walk along the beach—anywhere where you can see the last rays of the day fade to darkness. For your feast, pack an easy dinner—a Chinese chicken salad or a ham and cheese quiche, and a beverage to enjoy in the good company of friends, family, or yourself.

> *Easy Salad Dinners*: I called my good friend Nancy for her great Chinese chicken recipe. She laughed and told me it was a prepackaged kit found at most grocery stores. Well—if it tastes good and is easy to make, it works in my book.

Summertime Fun

During the summer months, pick one night a week (or more) and announce that it is officially "BBQ night." Delegate and rotate tasks so everyone helps with the meal and enjoys the evening spent outdoors. Several years ago, we invested in a portable fire pit and by now have lost count of the great times we've had around it with friends and family.

Picnic Italiano

Antipasto, the Italian term for cold *hors d'oeuvres,* is derived from the word *pasto* (meal) with the Latin prefix *ante* (before). The next time that you pack a moveable feast, borrow this Italian appetizer idea and serve it for dinner instead. In your basket, add a round loaf of crusty bread, various cheeses, fresh fruit, sliced deli meats, a marinated cold pasta and vegetable salad, and a jar of imported *Cerignola* olives.

With *biscotti* for dessert and a thermos of coffee (decaf if you're caffeine sensitive), you will have the makings of a wonderful meal to enjoy outside.

Tortellini Salad with Sundried Tomato Pesto and Pepperoni by Theresa Lichtenfels
Pesto:

- 3 tbsp. Dijon mustard
- 4 gloves garlic
- 1 tbsp. fennel seeds
- 1 jar sundried tomatoes (7 oz.)
- 1½ cups olive oil
- 2 tbsp. fresh lemon juice
- Add ingredients to food processor and blend until smooth.

Salad:

- 2 lbs cheese- or meat-filled tortellini (cooked and drained)
- ¼ lb sliced pepperoni
- 2 ripe tomatoes, chopped
- 1 yellow bell pepper, diced
- ½ cup chopped fresh parsley
- 3 tbsp. chopped fresh basil

Toss the first five ingredients with the pesto dressing, sprinkle the herbs over the top and garnish with black olives. Serves 8 to 10.

Spitting Allowed

For your next backyard picnic, buy a seeded watermelon and make eating it a play session. Adults are invited, too. Since watermelon is 92 percent water, you will slurp a portion of your daily intake of water with each big, juicy slice. A two-cup serving delivers fifteen to twenty milligrams of lycopene, an antioxidant that helps reduce the risks of certain cancers.

Easy Dessert: Cherries are another fresh idea for dessert at a picnic where spitting is encouraged.

Motivational Titles

To involve your whole family in the planning and preparation of a picnic, use any of these motivating titles:

Cruise Director: In charge of planning the afternoon's activities and packing the required items for fun.

Chef Extraordinaire: Responsible for bringing all the necessary grilling utensils and to follow through with the duties bestowed upon the grill master.

Edible Containers:

Peppers: Use green, red, yellow, or orange peppers. Wash and cut off the tops, remove seeds, and fill with your favorite dip.

Avocados: Cut in half, remove pit, and scoop out of skin. In a bowl, mash the avocado with fresh pressed garlic and a bit of salsa to taste, and garnish with generous squirts of lemon (to keep your festive dip from browning). Fill both halves of the avocado shell and top with half of the pit—rumored from international kitchens to keep your dip from losing its fresh green color.

Red Cabbage: Hollow out the middle, balance it between other solid vegetables on the tray, and fill it up with ranch dressing or hummus.

Round Bread Loaf: Scoop out the center of the bread, cube it for dipping in spinach and sour cream dip. Add chopped water chestnuts to give the dip a unique crunch.

Melons: Select a watermelon, cantaloupe, Persian, Casaba, canary, honeydew, or Crenshaw melon. Cut the fruit in half. Use a melon baller to scoop bite-sized morsels from both halves. Fill one half with fruit and use the empty other half as a lid to transport your ready-made dessert. Use your "fruit bowl" to hold other fruit such as berries or fill it with scoops of vanilla ice cream straight from the ice cream maker.

Prep Chef: Must be handy with a knife and efficient with filling the least number of Tupperware containers to go with prepped and marinated ingredients. Also ensures the picnic basket is replenished and ready to go at all times.

Logistics Specialist: Accepts the challenge of how to make everything fit in the prescribed space of the

Melons contain the compound adenosine, also found in garlic. Since it acts as an anticoagulant to help thin the blood, including both at your picnics regularly can help lessen the risk of heart attack and stroke.

car, including chairs, paper goods and/or linens, and other necessary goodies: flashlights, glow sticks, sidewalk chalk, kites, Wiffle ball and bat.

Lunch in the Park

Summer music festivals, in particular free concerts sponsored by local towns and cities, are always an excellent excuse to pack a picnic basket—even if you forgo the preparation recommended by some domestic goddesses. Whether your picnic is made at home or by the grocery store, either way you still get to relish the warm afternoon sun, lounge past the edge of twilight, or cuddle while waiting for the moon to make its appearance. This is one guaranteed way to bring peace and tranquility to any day and is a must in the summer.

In this lifetime, make it a goal to travel to some of these first-rate summer concerts and not only see new places but enjoy these wonderful sounds at this time of year. Let the music encourage you to explore the world outside.

Summer Party Games: Pick partners and start a water-balloon-toss contest. Want more laughs? Use hardboiled eggs and slip one raw egg into the game. On a particularly hot day, pass out the squirt guns, pick teams, and go into hiding. After half an hour, the least soggy team wins. You might want to issue eye protection or order that only hits from the waist down count to avoid accidents. Three-legged races, potato-sack race, eat the gummy worm off the string (similar to the donut game, but replace with worms), wheelbarrow race—you get the idea. Anything goes!

Picnic Packages: Many prepackaged foods contain monosodium glutamate (MSG), a common food-flavor enhancer, so be aware what you are packing in your picnic. Check the label for MSG—you may want to choose an alternative brand.

Boating Days

Find a boat: rent one or pull your dusty one out of the garage. Don't have one? Suggest a boating-party idea to a friend with a boat and promise to bring the picnic. Theme your open-water banquet to match your mood and appetite: a huge Greek salad with a side of stuffed grape leaves and cold meatballs, Spicy Thai Peanut Chicken wraps in spinach tortillas, Asian beef and noodle bowls, or *stromboli* served with crudités and a balsamic vinegar dipping sauce. This afternoon, decide to visit whatever foreign land on your boat via your taste buds.

The Sounds of Summer:
- Newport, Rhode Island: *Newport Music Festival*
- Katonah, New York: *Caramoor's International Music Festival*
- Big Boulders, Pennsylvania: *Poconos Blues Summer Festival*
- Charlottesville, Virginia: *Charlottesville Chamber Music Festival*
- Boone, North Carolina: *An Appalachian Summer Festival*
- Charleston, South Carolina: *Spoleto Festival USA*
- Orlando, Florida: *All American Music Festival*
- Aspen, Colorado: *Aspen Music Festival*
- Steamboat Springs, Colorado: *Strings in the Mountains*
- San Diego, Califorina: *SummerFest La Jolla*

Autumn Tailgating Picnics

Whenever I hear the word *tailgating*, I immediately think of my collegiate days spent in a blustery parking lot sipping a hot beverage and eating from the row of food displayed from the back of a car. Great friends and great food around a sporting game always ensured a great time no matter what the weather. Now I use the term a bit more broadly and encourage you to do the same.

Whether it is an afternoon spent at the baseball field, poolside at a swim meet, a tennis tournament, or frisbee at the park, there are many excuses to recreate the fun and social atmosphere of a great tailgating party.

Send the word to the other moms and dads to meet you in the parking lot after the kid's game with their portable grills, lawn chairs, and favorite dish to share. While the grill heats up, toast the winning team with lemonade. No need to cook dinner tonight—this afternoon will automatically extend into the later hours of evening with everyone having such a good time. Maybe this tailgating party should be a weekly event…

Perfect Picnic Sandwich by Nicole Guyot

Slice the top off a large Italian square bread (foccacia). Spread the bottom with aïoli and layer with deli luncheon meats—salami, pepperoni, ham, and/or prosciutto—and a variety of cheeses—smoked mozzarella, provolone, and Gouda. Drain a jar of peppers or marinated asparagus and add to your sandwich creation. Replace the "lid" to your picnic sandwich and wrap in clear plastic wrap. Let sit in the refrigerator for at least six hours or make the day before. Place at the bottom of the picnic basket to *ensure* this sandwich gets squished. Cut in thin strips and serve. This is a perfect sandwich for a picnic basket.

Autumn Party Games: Build a big bonfire and take turns telling ghost stories. Encourage wild imaginations and award the tallest tales with prizes of s'mores and other sweet treats.

Wintertime Fun

The national park's day-use areas are set up perfectly for winter picnics and are just waiting for you to visit and enjoy the beauty of a winter wonderland. Dig out the cross-country skis or snowshoes to discover in a new fun way the walking path used frequently during the summer. We did this one winter at Hahn's Peak Lake and had a great time. We parked on the street and skied or snowshoed a mile or so to the pavilion area that had grills—buried in snow, but still available for our use.

The tallest member of our snow-picnic crew carried the matches and charcoal on his back. Our second in command—associate grill master—carried the hot dogs and fixings. I took care of bringing the hot drinks and marshmallows. The others dragged plastic sleds behind them, which carried the paper goods, newspaper, kindling, tarp, and shovel—and once emptied, we test drove the sleds on a new sledding knoll next to the picnic tables.

Winter Picnic Games: Pack a plastic saucer, sled, toboggan, or ice skates for hours of delightful screams of joy. Winter play is ideal for all ages, and you are never too old to join in on the fun. Build an ice castle and defend your palace—a snowball battle will soon ensue.

O Christmas Tree

This holiday season, pack up the family and invite the neighbors, too, for a hike in a winter wonderland. Rent snowshoes, bring a tarp, ropes, a sharp saw, and remember to obtain a permit from your local Parks and Recreation department for cutting down a Christmas tree. (In Colorado, it costs ten dollars.) This family tradition is great for any age. Don't forget the camera and be sure to call everyone early to get this fun outing on the calendar.

Leave a thermos or two of hot chocolate, cider, or tea, and chili, and a box of holiday cookies in the car for your celebration of discovering the perfect tree. Use a cooler to keep the hot foods hot and the room temperature snacks from freezing—you want to reward, not disappoint your workers.

One year we went out the Saturday after Thanksgiving to burn those calories consumed on fat Thursday. Last year, our tree-hunting party had to use snowshoes to get to our treasure, which we had marked two weeks prior to Christmas.

If a national forest is not in your backyard, still make an outing of finding the perfect Christmas tree. To conclude your successful shopping at the local corner lot selling precut trees, pack a Christmas tree tailgating picnic. Whatever way a Christmas tree is found this year, the time spent together will continue to top your family's list of fun memories.

In Holland, it is common to see many cross-country ice skaters enjoying winter on the frozen canals. They ice skate many kilometers up and down these perfect lanes for hours of wintertime play. Local pubs welcome these winter enthusiasts with rubber mats leading from the ice avenues to their front door so they can warm up and enjoy something warm to eat and drink.

On the Road across America

Before your next road trip, allow yourself an extra half-hour to pack a car picnic. Tea sandwiches cut into bite-sized triangles permit the kids and even the driver to eat without a mess.

Wrap each sandwich in plastic wrap and then enclose in a cloth napkin to serve as a "lap cloth" while eating this decadent yet simple lunch. Better yet—toss a picnic blanket in the car and stop for a while to enjoy the fresh lunch and your company.

In a thermos, bring along freshly brewed Darjeeling, Assam, or Sencha tea and wrap up a few ginger cookies for dessert. Surprise the little ones with a seasonal drink, too—fruit punch, chocolate milk, hot cocoa, or cider.

Travel Aromatherapy: When traveling by plane to a party or celebration, here are a few ways to arrive feeling together rather than out of sorts:

- Essence of peppermint will refresh the air of a stuffy car—and you.
- Drink a glass of ginger ale or ginger tea to ease motion sickness.
- Gingersnaps and ginger candies can also help remedy this malady.

Diner Talk

During the 1930s and '40s, "blue-plate" specials served at diners were originally inexpensive

Happy Sandwiches:

- Egg salad topped with fresh green romaine lettuce and bacon on dark rye.
- Fresh buffalo mozzarella cheese layered between a fresh basil leaf and a slice of red ripe tomato on sourdough bread.
- Smoked turkey with avocado slices or cranberry jelly on hearty wheat. Use lettuce to keep the soft ingredients from soaking the bread.
- Gourmet PBJs with either smooth or crunchy peanut butter and your favorite jam.

meals made from leftovers. Today this popular dish still served at refurbished diners
or brand new cafés with neon lights and
shiny red booths means the "dish of the day"
or "specialty of the house."

> "SOS," otherwise known as chipped beef
> on toast, was served during World War II
> to soldiers who returned home to find it
> being served as a blue-plate special. For
> some, it is still comfort food.

Window Seats

Long ago, while on a lengthy road trip from
Southern California to Portland, Oregon, my husband and I tired of eating at restaurants
and craved to be out of the car and buildings.

We discovered a small seafood market on the back roads near Coos Bay, Oregon. I
looked at my husband as he turned into the market's dirt parking lot and immediately
knew the answer to "What's for dinner?"

We purchased shrimp, clams, and a loaf of crusty French bread. From our cooler and
camping box, we had the other ingredients and tools to create a gourmet meal. We climbed
down a steep cliff to a private cove to select our window seat by the ocean.

Appetizers consisted of a fresh green salad—ingredients also offered at the seafood
market—and a slice of the tasty bread. A small fire cooked our seafood feast. We packaged
the shrimp with a splash of beer in a foil boat and watched for the clams to open on the
grill borrowed from our camp stove, directly above the heat from the ash-white
driftwood.

We knew our seafood dinner would have cost at least triple the amount we had spent at
the fine restaurant that we had passed on the bluff, and knowing this, we enjoyed our dinner at the edge of the water immensely.

Look for ways to make any of your trips down the road memorable. You might even pick
up new culinary skills along the way to try on the backyard BBQ.

Island Tales

This year, follow your taste buds on your quest to discover excellent regional foods.

The San Juan Islands are one of the best places in the world to experience fresh saltwater oysters—delectable delicacies from the icy blue waters. For a show by the talented shucker, pull up a seat at the oyster bar. As he pries open an oyster for you to try, he will entertain you with stories from the sea.

I had had raw oysters on the half shell before visiting Orcas Island, but not like this. With a comforting ocean breeze blowing in off the dock, the salty taste of the air, each oyster was like tasting the sea.

If you find yourself searching for a peaceful retreat this summer, or better yet in the early days of autumn, then set your sails on Orcas, Lopez, or Shaw island and enjoy the plentiful and delicious berries, shellfish, and of course, oysters.

Prior to refrigeration, the adage was that oysters were to be taken from the sea only during the months that end in the letter "r." This rule only worked for the Northern Hemisphere. Nowadays with oysters and other shellfish being shipped overnight from all over the world, these delicacies from the sea are available year-round depending upon where they are harvested.

Stories from the Road

Did you ever wonder why chicken wings are called buffalo wings? I did and thought you should know, too— just in case anyone ever asks you. Here is the story:

In 1964, Teresa Bellissimo, owner of the Anchor Bar in Buffalo, New York, was faced with the dilemma of

Supersize It? If you said "Yes," you may have just ordered a total of 1,610 calories all in one meal:
Big Mac = 590 calories
Supersize French fries = 610 calories
and a Supersize Coca-Cola (42 oz.) = 410 calories.

The idea of serving a salad with dinner is a twentieth-century invention. Leafy green vegetables did turn up at the dinner table in previous centuries, but in the form of coleslaw or swimming in soups.

having to use up an oversupply of chicken wings. So with a little improvising, a lot of hot sauce, and a bit of blue-cheese dressing to cool the bite, this entrepreneur had a success on her hands as well as a new appetizer on the menu.

Do you enjoy a Caesar salad from time to time? Ever wonder what the story was behind the naming of those tantalizing tasty greens and its secret dressing? Is this impossibly popular salad named after the Roman head of state himself? The Caesar salad is actually named after Caesar Cardini, an Italian immigrant with a chain of restaurants in Tijuana, Mexico. His refreshing salad became so popular with the Hollywood jet set, which frequented his eating places south of San Diego, they began to order it by saying, "I'll have one of Caesar's salads."

Advice from the Restaurant Table

According to local Parisian history, a plaque inscribed in Latin hung above the door of one of the first restaurants on the *Rue des Poules*: "*Venite ad me omnes qui stomacho laboratis et ego restaurabo vos,*" that is, "Come, all ye that labor on your stomach, and I shall restore you."

Some Chinese restaurants, unless noted on the menu, add MSG to their dishes. You can ask them not to.

On the road for business, pleasure, or simply as a stop between here and where you are going, you have permission to eat. Taste everything, but exert balance. Save room to have dessert, a second glass of your favorite beverage, or chocolate!

When you do overindulge, simply add additional time to play to even out intake of calories with the output of energy the next day or over the next couple of days.

Twelve Dining-Out Tips:
1. Eat half of the entrée and request the rest to be packaged to go.
2. Request broiled meats or vegetarian meals.
3. Order an appetizer for dinner or split an entrée.
4. Start with soup or a salad.
5. Ask for salad dressing on the side. Use a teaspoon to add the dressing according to taste, not eye appeal. You will be surprised how a little can go a long way.
6. Try a plain baked potato with chives or add plain yogurt or ketchup as a topping.
7. Order steamed vegetables and squeeze a lemon wedge to bring out the flavors.
8. Substitute tomato slices for french fries.
9. Frequent ethnic restaurants that steam or stir-fry their entrées.
10. Share desserts or select fresh fruit, sorbet, sherbet, or angel food cake instead.
11. Cancel the free refills and request water instead.
12. Go for a walk before getting back in the car.

According to the University of Arkansas, we can live six weeks without food but no more than one week without water.

Conversational Tidbit: The after-dinner mint, generally presented with the bill, was originally meant to have customers leave with a sweet taste in their mouths.

The National Restaurant Association reported the biggest moneymaker now in restaurant sales are from the purchase of larger dining plates. Over the last decade, America's dinner plate increased from eight- to nine-inch plates to a ten- to fourteen-inch spread in which to load up; nowadays the norm is a whopping twelve-inch platter.

> **Manhattan is a narrow island off the coast of New Jersey devoted to the pursuit of lunch.**
> —*Raymond Sokolov (b. 1941)*

> **There's a pizza place near where I live that sells only slices. In the back, you can see a guy tossing a triangle in the air.**
> —*Steven Wright (b. 1955)*

Best of the Best

Each year, usually in the summer or autumn, cities across the United States host "best of the best" celebrations and gather together the best chefs and their restaurants for the public to sample.

Instead of waiting for this annual shenanigan, I say *why not venture out on your own search for the best of the best?* Will you take on the challenge of discovering which state or city makes the best apple pie? Where can you find the perfect pizza in America? Or what about the finest, finger-licking ribs?

Here is a story that might ignite your curiosity and interest to become a regular food critic. In search of the best pizza, my husband and I decided to taste-test pizza on our trip across the country—Los Angeles to Chicago to New York City. We waged a bet prior to the start of our little contest. I put my money on New York City to come up with the best pizza pie while my husband cast his vote for his favorite pizzeria in Los Angeles. To our surprise, after the fun of tasting many slices, Chicago's hand-tossed, cornmeal-crust pizza won. On the way back to Los Angeles, we threw in the betting kitty and bought a whole pizza in Chicago to celebrate.

Pizza Picnics

In the 1950s, Shakey's started the pizza craze in America, followed closely by Pizza Hut. Domino's, set up exclusively for delivery, offered pizza lovers the convenience of not having to cook or pick up. Little Caesar's and other regional pizza companies continue to offer consumers the accepted standard pizza pie. By the 1980s, pizza franchises substantially outnumbered hamburger chains, and their numbers did not include the frozen grocery-store pizza segment.

After fifty years, Americans have developed a strong passion and appetite for their pizza pies. Why not take your pizza outside tonight and call it a picnic? Remember, simplicity is key.

"U Pick" Signs

How and where do you start to journey about in this big world? It is easy. Follow your passions—they will lead to new worlds that you may never have thought of visiting before.

Think in color. What is your favorite? What is naturally made of this beautiful hue? Just by adding color to your diet, you may find a new road to travel. For example, just in the name of raspberries, you and a good friend could christen a new annual pilgrimage for this worthy fruit. Your time and energy will be well spent in an exhilarating road trip in search of these healthy berries.

Welcome the opportunity to sit on the ground and fill up your bucket. If you live on the East Coast, start in Maryland and track down the elusive yellow berries. In the south, drive to North Carolina and search for the celebrated lavender-colored raspberries. Extend your adventure, if time permits, and meander over to Alabama to where the pink varieties grow.

Every August, South Haven, Michigan, the self-proclaimed "National Blueberry Capital," hosts its annual blueberry festival—complete with a pie-eating contest. If you have never entered a pie-eating contest, this might be your invitation to give it a try. Why not? You only live once...(269) 637-5252.

Whoever thought the pursuit of a berry could have you traipsing across this great country of ours?

This July, you might want to set your traveling sights on Oregon. The reason? It is harvest time for the sweetest of all blackberries, Marionberries. First developed in the 1950s,

"U-Pick" signs still dot country roads, beckoning the gatherers down their lanes.

Enjoy Marionberries still warm from the afternoon sun or savor them later as the juicy fruit treat in scones, as a fresh topping on shortcake, in pies, cobblers, ice cream, cupcakes, muffins, or frozen in ice cubes with a sprig of mint floating in a tall glass of fresh-squeezed lemonade. Also great as a jam or pancake syrup, you will not have a hard time eating these local berries a different way every day.

Oregon also provides the opportunity on the West Coast to pick pink raspberries, and while on your berry-hunting adventure in this beautiful state be sure to track down the deep, wine-colored wild raspberries. White raspberries are plentiful in the wild, so keep your eyes open for this interesting alternative as well.

Back-Road Trips

Traverse the back roads of America to explore regional cuisine. Once this *al fresco* bug bites you, it might make it easier to detour more frequently off the beaten interstate in your quest to discover new fresh ingredients and tantalizing recipes to bring home for your next picnic.

Head to the green hills and pastures that deliver the peace and quiet you crave. Pack the car and head to Vermont or any other sleepy destination bathed in various shades of greens. Let its beauty fill you up again—from the new budded trees and wakening meadows covered in its first flowers to its meandering rivers and picturesque valleys.

Summer is a beautiful time of the year up in this northern state of ours and an especially great time to explore great ice cream made at the source. First stop: Ben & Jerry's ice cream factory in Waterbury. Or you could compare tastes at numerous dairy farms along your route that offer freshly churned ice cream and then vote on who makes the very best.

Afterward, be sure to include active play in your day to return your ice-cream stomach to normal. Hiking, biking, and swimming are good, fun-time family activities. You may even want to try paragliding or hot air ballooning over the Green Mountains as an inspiring way to get the creative juices flowing. Visit artist communities in Woodstock or Quechee or any of the summer fairs where handcrafted creations are for sale. Choose from oil and watercolor paintings and wood-carving sculptures to handmade quilts and jams, and of course, pure Grade A maple syrup. Drink in the serenades offered nightly at summer concerts. A week tucked away at a quiet inn or peaceful campground will return you to your daily life refreshed and recharged.

Southern Crossroads

If you don't choose carefully, car travel in the United States continues to offer the same tired food. The fast-food type of fuel wears not only the stomach but also the spirit. Veer off the freeway and travel the back roads to find a local eatery to taste some real home cooking and come home with a new picnic recipe.

When in the south, do as the southerners do—eat your blackened redfish, spicy Louisiana gumbo with okra, jambalaya made with duck or alligator, or a bowl of red beans and rice. Capture the deliciousness of a Creole dish, a fusion of French, Spanish, and African cuisines anywhere in the French Quarter.

Miles west of New Orleans, you might want to pause in Mississippi for a taste of their local cuisine—a Po' Boy sandwich—with your choice of shrimp, oyster, crayfish, or even alligator (tastes like chicken, but chewier).

Add a little Tabasco sauce, spicy Cajun music such as *Le Gran Mamou: A Cajun Music Anthology* and your picnic will be a lively feast.

Vast Spaces

The Coachella Valley of Indio, California, is responsible for 95 percent of the dates consumed in the United States. Every February since 1921, this bountiful basin, with a climate similar to that of the Sahara Desert, hosts a ten-day date festival. Some of the palms are Moroccan offshoots planted here in the early 1900s. At this celebration, be sure to sample a bit of all the offerings: a slice of date pie or date cake, a date shake, chocolate-covered dates, or a few date cookies, and pack a box of pure raw dates for the road.

European Excursions

Need an excuse to travel Europe? Take a tour of cities renowned for their cultivation of the finest wines, cheese, beer, or mustards and become a connoisseur about their regional pride and joy. Learn the history, types, and taste all of the various mustards throughout Germany and France. This jaunt alone could detain you in Europe for another month. Enjoy the taste-testing while riding around the quaint backcountry roads.

Hadley Fruit Orchards in Cabazon, California, has been offering an ample selection of fruits and nuts since 1931. Next time you visit Mickey Mouse, take a detour to the Palm Springs area to try a jumbo *Medjool*. One bite and you will know why these dates were once reserved for royalty.

Please Pass the Grey Poupon

For any mustard gourmand, a visit to Dijon in France is a must. Its reputation, exalted by the Dukes of Burgundy, has been firmly established since the fourteenth century and does not waver from its prestigious standard today. However, there are those who argue that only the mustard crafted in Düsseldorf, Germany, can be the best suited for German sausages.

In 1752, Maille, a recognized name among true mustard aficionados, developed twenty-four mustard varieties, including red mustards and fine mustards made with garlic, tarragon, fine herbs, and even lemon (as well as ninety-two vinegars).

Bordin, his contemporary, created forty different mustards, including varieties flavored with champagne, mushrooms, roses, and vanilla.

Of course, on your way between the countries make sure to continue your taste-testing and sample other true fripperies—wine, beer, and cheese—native to these lands. You can always do a comparative test back on U.S. soil in Napa and Sonoma. Get together with friends and call this investigation of regional specialties a party.

The Yellow Party

Invite everyone to bring an old-time favorite mustard or a brand new one to try in the company of adventurous friends. Serve the right foods in order to taste-test the various mustards on the correct food item: hot dogs, *kielbasa,* and pretzels, both soft and hard.

Let the party cast their vote for the English, German, or American mustard, or jars that hail from Bordeaux or Dijon. Perhaps the crowd will prefer herb, Champagne, Beaujolais, or mustard made with whole mustard seeds, beer, chilies, or honey. This tasting party could be your answer to what to do at the next tailgating party.

Always a Picnic

No matter where you have to go each day, be sure to welcome beauty and peace into your life. Nature offers us tranquility for free. To make sure some part of your day is spent outside, up and away from the usual bustle, pack a picnic. These moveable feasts are essential and need to be included in the many meals consumed during a lifetime.

Where are you going to go today to brighten one of your dining hours?

Black Bean and Corn Salad by Laura Stout
  2 cans of black beans (15 oz. each), drained
  1 bag of frozen whole-kernel corn (10 oz.), defrosted
  ½ large red pepper, chopped
  ½ red onion, chopped
  ¼ cup loosely packed chopped cilantro
Dressing:
  ¼ cup rice wine vinegar
  2 tbsp. lime juice
  ½ cup extra virgin olive oil
  ½ tsp. cumin
  ¼ tsp. cayenne pepper
  ½ tsp. salt (or to taste)
Combine ingredients with salad dressing. Serve as a side salad, use to top your favorite grilled fish, or mix with equal parts of salsa and present as an alternative Mexican chip dip.

chapter 8

parties
FOR TWO

 scrumptious secrets

> Romeo, Romeo! Wherefore art thou Romeo?
> —*William Shakespeare (c. 1564–1616)*

For centuries, love potions, amulets, spells involving food, and charms have been used by people from all over the world to spice up their love lives. Recipes found in Asia, Africa, Europe, the Middle East, and Latin and North America attest to this quest for undying love. Ironically, monks were infamous for creating liqueurs with aphrodisiac qualities, including Chartreuse, Benedictine, and Frangelica, to name the more recognizable potions still in production today.

In 1044, a monk originally from Normandy created an elixir with dried earthworms and periwinkle flowers for the altar wine. This powerful love spell resulted in a population boom, and France could no longer hold all of its citizens. An invasion of England followed in 1066 to allow for the settlement of the new families.

During the fourth century BC, Theophrastus, a Greek botanist, recommended a love potion that contained the leafy plant called mandrake soaked in vinegar to create the sensation of feeling high. This popular beverage sold out quickly among the party-loving populous.

Ancient Indian recipes for love were enhanced with the ingredients of black pepper, chili, honey, and peppers. Mandrake worked equally well in these love recipes, as it had for the Greeks.

Periwinkle, one of the most potent of all flowers used in witchcraft, was christened with its own folk name, "Sorcerer's Violet."

Sweet Secrets: Hershey's Chocolate Kisses are called "kisses" because they are made on a conveyor belt that looks as though it is being kissed by the machine that shapes the candies.

The first known cookbook author, Apicius, who lived during the reign of Julius Caesar, offered the love remedy of a stew cooked with onions, pine kernels, and various secretive herbs.

The good news is that the list of aphrodisiacs is long. The bad news is not everyone agrees about the powers possessed by spices, herbs, fruits, vegetables, seafood, and, of course, chocolate. Explore the world of romantic possibilities on your own terms and expectations. Sample whatever piques your heart and appetite. No harm in savoring a bit of chocolate in the name of research.

Chocolate contains more than four hundred different chemicals, including phenylethylamine (PEA), an amphetamine-like brain chemical that triggers the sense of euphoria experienced when people fall in love. In addition, the combination of fat and sugar increases the natural pleasure chemicals produced by the brain called endorphins. With the stimulants theobromine and caffeine, which revs the nervous system and elevates the heart rate, it is no wonder women crave this indulgence, and many claim it to be a guaranteed love charm.

Scrumptious Secrets

Until the advent of cookbooks, the belief in food superstitions, myths, age-old rituals, customs, and traditions usually kept most guests around the table alive. Other tales fueled the already larger-than-life fables surrounding infamous lovers and their feats, encouraged the brave to tempt fate and try their first raw oyster, the leaves of prickly artichokes, and cooked spinach. But in the name of a party, and this is a party for two, anything goes, or as in earlier cases of food preparation, if believed, it will come true in love matters.

Love Flowers: Bees feast upon the heather flower to produce a dark and tangy honey. Look for this variety at your natural food store. Honey is the only food that does not spoil, and therefore logic says it can then be kept in any room. Cleopatra is said to have had honey in every room of the palace.

> **A life of abundance comes only through great love.**
> —*Elbert Hubbard (1856–1915)*

Love Vegetables

Prior to the 1500s, French women were forbidden to eat artichokes, a reputed aphrodisiac. However, Queen Catherine de Médici was very fond of the vegetable and encouraged its cultivation, much to the relief of many male Parisians.

After eating this love veggie, the artichoke, various medical studies show the patient's blood cholesterol level drops. The anti-cholesterol drug, cynara, a derivative of this vegetable, continues to support these positive medical findings.

Tonight, serve this finger-licking food at your party for two. It just might end up in a win-win situation for both hearts. If this is not a reason to celebrate, I do not know what is.

The Chinese believe that eating asparagus increases feelings of compassion and love.

This superstition may not be too far removed from the truth. The vegetable's root contains the compound *steroidal glycoside* that directly affects hormone production.

Steam and serve asparagus cold, sprinkled with a few sesame seeds (recognized to possess magic and aid in the love department). In addition to the white sesame seeds used in the kitchens of the United States, black sesame seeds are popular in Japan and China. These tiny seeds are just as tasty as the lighter colored variety. Arrange the asparagus on a bed of butter or red-leaf lettuce, add pinwheels of cooked, cooled carrots, and serve with a sweet soy, rice vinegar, and fresh ginger sauce. This tricolor recipe, provided by Beth the Chef of Steamboat Springs, provides yet another excellent way to get your servings of vegetables—and possibly love—tonight.

Prior to Popeye's time, folklore included spinach in its repertoire of miracle foods with its promise to restore energy, increase vitality, and improve the quality of one's blood.

Spinach contains about twice as much iron as other leafy greens and is also rich in beta-carotene, vitamin E, folic acid, vitamin B6, choline, vitamin C, calcium, magnesium, phosphorus, potassium, manganese, zinc, chromium, iodine, and nickel.

My suggestion is to layer spinach into lasagna, add it to an omelet, blend it into a veggie beverage with carrots, celery, and tomatoes, or use the fresh leaves in place of pasta and top with a hearty beef and green pepper marinara sauce.

> *Easy Appetizer*: Lightly rub an artichoke with extra virgin olive oil. Mince garlic and place between the leaves. Steam for thirty to forty minutes and enjoy naked—that is without butter, margarine, or mayonnaise. To use these condiments would only counteract the benefits of this heart-healthy aphrodisiac.

> **I'm strong to the finish 'cause I eats me spinach.**
> —*Popeye the Sailor Man, created by Elzie Segar (1894–1938)*

My favorite recipe for this leafy green is to create a fresh spinach salad. Top with sliced hardboiled eggs, halved seedless red grapes, raw red onion circles, and finish with a handful of chopped walnuts.

> To love someone deeply gives you strength. Being loved by someone deeply gives you courage.
> —*Lao Tzu (c. 600 BC)*

Don Juan's Secret

The common onion, once prescribed by herbalists because of its perceived powers to restore sexual potency, is still used frequently in the cooking pots of the Italians, Spanish, and French. This may indeed be Romeo's, Casanova's, and Don Juan's long-held love secret…

Add this bulb—sliced, diced, or minced—to your intimate party dish for two. You, too, might become a staunch believer in this legendary allium.

If serving a hearty Italian dish topped with the regulatory love portion of onions (and garlic—more on this wonder love drug next), you may also want to present your special guest with a few cloves to chew on while awaiting dessert—and you.

Love Bulbs

The Egyptians worshipped garlic, Greeks hated it, and Romans cooked almost everything with it. In Provence, France, the breezy air is saturated with the heady mouth-watering aroma of cooking garlic.

According to the *Journal of the National Cancer Institute* (November 2002) another reason to get the man in your life to eat his allium vegetables—onions, shallots, garlic, chives, and leeks—is that a serving of at least ten grams a day reduces his chance of prostate cancer.

Before Certs: Ancient Chinese literature reveals an ingenious custom of those who reported directly to the emperor. According to references within the manuscripts, these courtiers and officers of the state usually kept a few cloves in their mouths to keep their breath and perhaps the news—good and bad—sweet.

From California's Interstate 5 freeway forty-three miles away, you can smell the garlic growing in the sun-drenched fields surrounding Gilroy. If passing by in July, make a detour when the entire town cooks and bakes with its famed love vegetable at its annual festival. This self-proclaimed "Garlic Capital of the World" celebrates this humble herb in so many different ways that you will be overwhelmed in the decision of what to try first.

> **Garlic is as good as ten mothers.**
> —*Les Blank (b. 1935)*

> **There is no such thing as a little garlic.**
> —*Arthur "Bugs" Baer (1886–1969)*

From garlic scampi, garlic-seasoned calamari, stir-fried vegetables with garlic, garlic-infused sirloin, garlic pasta, and baked elephant garlic, to garlic bread and garlic ice cream, here is an opportunity to test first-hand if garlic is truly an aphrodisiac.

Food Superstitions and Other Myths

When we reach the point when our food is truly tasted and not simply inhaled, then we can call ourselves pure gourmands. Venture on a mysterious and mouth-watering excursion to discover the love powers of foods, herbs, and spices, and possibly make up your own myths.

What else could possibly be needed for complete satisfaction?

The argument for all centuries is whether or not the mushroomlike truffle is an aphrodisiac. The debate continues in spite of proof that eating it does make women more loving and men more lovable.

"The truffle is the diamond of cookery," says Brillat-Savarin, author of *Physiology of Taste*. Add truffle shavings to your romantic dish for two tonight; this decadent ingredient just might be worth the cost and most likely, worthy of your intentions.

Routt County, Colorado: Every May, the nonprofit organization Yampatika hosts a Wild Edible Feast with local botanist Karin Vail, who takes a hardworking crew into nature to harvest the herbs, flowers, and roots that will make the menu for this delectable evening.

Edible Flowers: Nasturtiums taste peppery like watercress. Carnations are tasty, but be sure to cut off the bitter base of the flower. Petunias, violets, calendula (or marigolds, the poor man's saffron), clover, dandelion leaves, the petals of gladioli, and lavender add wonderful new aromas, color, and flavor to soups, salads, and desserts.

Love Oils

During the heydays of the Greeks, the olive was so respected that only those who took a vow of chastity were permitted to take part in the harvest.

> The olive tree is surely the richest gift of heaven.
> —*Thomas Jefferson (1743–1826)*

The only olive oil that can be labeled "extra virgin" is the oil pressed once during extraction without any chemicals or extenders of other oils. Check the label to confirm your bottle of extra virgin olive oil is indeed what it claims to be; only those with an acidity of one percent or less can be virgin.

High in vitamins E, K, and numerous polyphenols, olive oil provides a defense mechanism to help the body delay the aging process, prevents cancers, arteriosclerosis, liver disorders, and inflammations. Add this beauty oil to your shopping list today and maintain your youthfulness from the inside.

Forbidden Fruits

On the island of Sri Lanka, an Indian legend tells of the Adam and Eve story with a different twist. The duo is banished from the Garden of Eden not

Massage Oils: Almond, grapeseed, jojoba, or sunflower oil are my top picks to use for massage. Scent with your favorite essential oils, but just a few drops. Less is more with these powerful essences.

because of eating the forbidden fruit, the apple—but the banana. In this area of the world, illustrations show the couple wearing only banana leaves.

The forbidden apple originated in Asia Minor and later grew wildly popular in Europe due to the belief that this fruit was an aphrodisiac.

> **Life without love is a tree without blossom and fruit.**
> —*Kahlil Gibran (1883–1931)*

The symbolic fruits of the goddess Aphrodite include the quince, pomegranate, and apple.

The humble peach, originally from China, made its way to Persia and at one time was considered poisonous. Now consumed in enormous quantities, peaches are the second largest commercial fruit crop in the States, second only to apples, and are eaten everywhere, including other countries that are major producers: Italy, China, and Greece. Peaches now are even enjoyed in Persia.

With more than five thousand different types of pears available throughout the world, the more recognizable ones to U.S. residents include Bartlett, Anjou, Bosc, and Seckel—all a great source for fiber, vitamin C, and calcium. The pear, a favorite erotic art subject because of its feminine shape, has a delicious taste as well as fragrance.

The Chinese consider peaches and apples to be erotic symbols.

Sexy Seeds and Herbs

From the same family as parsley, caraway has been used in cooking since medieval times. Love potions often included these curious seeds as a key ingredient. This warm and slightly bitter spice became popular in European and Jewish cooking. Women, perhaps wise to this seed's secret powers, generously added it to soups, fish, bread, and vegetables.

According to Isabel Allende's *Aphrodite, A Memoir of the Senses,* forbidden spices blacklisted by the Barefoot Sisters of the Poor included (a partial listing): cardamom, fenugreek, lavender, mustard, saffron, and turmeric.

Test this love theory tonight. Light the red tapers and set the table with the good linens and dishes. Serve a bowl of hearty soup and rustic rye bread laced with these mysterious seeds.

Who says dinner has to be complicated, especially when other activities should take precedence?

Color Tip: Red is the color of passion, said to stimulate conversation and excite the nervous system and senses.

Love enters a man through his eyes and a woman through her ears.
—*Italian proverb*

Traces of Temptations

In Europe, fenugreek is thought to provoke sensual dreams and ignite passion. Fenugreek, also known as *trigonella foenum-graecum,* is one of the oldest known medicinal plants, dating back to the ancient Egyptians and Hippocrates. This spice, with an aroma similar to celery, is good to eat cooked or lightly dry roasted and is a good source of vitamins, minerals, and protein—important in any diet, especially vegetarian. While considered to be a popular folk remedy for the common cold and raspy throats, it is also considered to be an aphrodisiac.

Maybe you should keep fenugreek handy in your spice rack. Brew a pot of fenugreek tea as a preventative measure to abate colds, clogged ears, and aching sinuses. Who can think about love when saddled with a head cold?

What did one do with fenugreek? I didn't know, nor did anyone else, but we all had a bottle of it, we apprentice gourmets, in our spice racks.
—*Mary Cantwell (1930–2000)*

Matchmakers of past centuries bet their business on the spice of coriander. Deemed an effective aphrodisiac, discreet women sprinkled the ground herb undetected into salsa and served it liberally to the unsuspecting guest. Perhaps contemporary women could stand to gain satisfactory results by borrowing from such customs of yesteryear.

> Fenugreek is native to the eastern Mediterranean and means "Greek hay."

Sweet Scents

Madame Pompadour used vanilla to perfume her clothing, which became the rage in Victorian England and in the New World. By the 1950s, American women dabbed a splash of the essence behind their ears to be as sweet as dessert.

> In 1874, vanillin, the first synthetic version of vanilla, was created from the sapwood found in certain conifers.

Vanilla is one of the world's most expensive spices; therefore the majority of the flavoring available on the open market, especially in the United States, is synthetic. When using the "essence" for perfume, purchase exactly that. Your nose, and perhaps your guest, will know the difference.

Allures from Paradise

According to Greek legend, Aphrodite, the goddess of love, gave her name to all the foods and potions that stirred the soul. The Romans called her Venus. Sandro Botticelli depicts her born on the foam of the sea in his masterpiece, *Birth of Venus,* painted circa 1485. Thus seafood in general—abalone, caviar, clams, mussels, sea urchins, and especially oysters—is said to be an aphrodisiac.

Stories about the lustful powers gleaned from seafood range from unbelievable to very well possible and true. Casanova, the legendary Latin lover, purportedly ate platters of oysters each day to be able to appease his consorts.

The insatiable demands of guests at Roman festivities required the host to send away as far as the English Channel for these delicacies. Packed in snow and ice, slaves carried the oysters over the land.

The eating of caviar dates back to antiquity; however, it was the poor fishermen who ate it. Royalty and other governing officials only wanted the best, so the roe had to be removed from the sturgeon in order to sell the fish.

Oysters are high in zinc, a mineral necessary for male virility.

In Chile, the tradition of eating "à la oyster" (or raw eggs) is said to incite virility and mend the body and memory after a heavy night of drinking.

As I ate the oysters with their strong taste of the sea and their faint metallic taste that the cold white wine washed away, leaving only the sea taste and the succulent texture, and as I drank their cold liquid from each shell and washed it down with the crisp taste of the wine, I lost the empty feeling and began to be happy, and to make plans.
—*Ernest Hemingway (1899–1961)*

Party of Two

To keep the fires alive, you need to feed the flames. Here are several ideas to get you thinking in the right direction of love and passion even if the laundry is not done and the dishes are still in the sink. Life goes by quickly and is very short indeed. Remember what will be important at the end of your life…

> ## I thought that spring must last forevermore, for I was young and loved, and it was May.
> —*Vera Brittain (1893–1970)*

Party Game: Savor all the possibilities of a fine love meal without seeing it first. With a trusted partner, let your tongue discover sour, sweet, bitter, astringent, and salty. Call the event a romantic celebration of food just between you two. Blindfold required.

Invitations for Love

Recreate a former date or weekend away without leaving home. Call up the restaurant or bed and breakfast and ask them to mail a brochure, a pack of matches, business card—some form of collateral from the romantic site, or check to see if they have a website and print notes from it. Are you talented in the kitchen? Make a meal from the menu of your favorite restaurant. These visual clues may be enough to ignite a trip down memory lane with your partner again.

Love Eras

When was your love life at its highest point? Was it the sock hops of the fifties, during the dancing seventies, or the big eighties? Purchase (or borrow) a disco ball and an album by the Bee Gees. Get out the turntable and relive those moments. Let music transport you back to this place and time of passion.

Did sharing an ice-cream soda make your heart flutter and palms sweat? Go in search of a soda-fountain counter and share these precious moments once again. Do whatever you can to remind both of you of these earlier, hotter times.

Massage Lessons

Learn the art of massage through books, videos, classes, or practice for free. Together, shop for essential oils, then go home and mix up a batch of alluring fragrances. Turn your home into a spa resort for the day. Enforce a strict dress code of bathrobes and slippers only. Turn off any lights and turn on the sounds of relaxing music. Focus only on each other.

Touch Test: **When purchasing pajamas, bathrobes, sheets, and lingerie, shop by touch. Avoid scratchy and synthetic fabrics for any tactile comforts to be worn next to your skin.**

Love Flowers: The word for pansy in French is *pensée* meaning "thought." It is believed that, when attending to the plucked bloom, you can hear your lover's thoughts.

Aromatherapy Tips: Rely on the pure essence of jasmine, ylang-ylang, rose, vanilla, sandalwood, or patchouli to make any day seem like Valentine's Day.

Romantic Music

To discover the world's most romantic music, spend an hour or two listening to sample tracks at your local music store. Take turns listening to each other's choice and decide on one or two new CDs for your love collection. Every day in the evening hours, play these persuasive lyrics.

Sweet Dates

Do not let the marked dates on the calendar—anniversaries, birthdays, Mother's Day, Father's Day, and Valentine's Day—be the only ones destined for romance. My suggestion is to practice on other days of the year with the aid of any one of these ready-to-go ideas to help spark a few dreamy evenings:

- *Party of two:* Present a gift-wrapped box of chocolate truffles and a romantic movie.
- *Under the covers:* Wrap a massage book inside a new bathrobe with a "Privacy Please" door sign tucked in the pocket.
- *Romantic picnic:* Fill a picnic basket to the brim with aphrodisiacs to sample and a book of love poetry.

Love Nuts: Almonds, known to the Romans as "Greek nuts," originated in Asia and were used to make soups as well as sweet desserts. Today, California supplies half of the world's crop, followed by Spain and Sicily.

Anniversary Ideas

Most women are familiar with the traditional and contemporary lists suggesting wedding anniversary gifts. Most men have probably never heard of such a shopping list.

For our sixth wedding anniversary almost a decade ago, I gave my husband a cord of wood. I had it delivered (all over the driveway), and to save the fifty-dollar stacking fee, told the company I would do it myself. It took a long while, but when my husband came home and saw his sweaty wife and the tall stack, he smiled. We had cozy fires in the backyard fire pit all year in Southern California together.

Since most of our wedding guests knew we were outdoor enthusiasts, most detoured to the sporting-goods store

Romantic Movies:
- *An Affair to Remember*
- *Casablanca*
- *Far and Away*
- *French Kiss*
- *Notting Hill*
- *Pride and Prejudice*
- *Singin' in the Rain*
- *Sleepless in Seattle*
- *Somewhere in Time*
- *Sweet Home Alabama*
- *The English Patient*
- *The Lover*
- *Wuthering Heights*

If a June night could talk, it would probably boast it invented romance.
—*Bernard Arthur Owen Williams (1929–2003)*

Cupid's Secrets: Fill your love repertoire with any of the following ingredients. Copy and place this list in his car for birthday, anniversary, and holiday gift ideas:

Lingerie: soft to touch, anything silk or 100 percent cotton, and easy to wear and remove

Robes: elegantly long, silky and short, or a thick and toasty option made of chenille or Turkish cotton

Pillows: unique shapes and sizes to provide support and comfort while spending many hours together

Bedding: romantic silk sheets and matching pillowcases—nothing else quite stirs the spirit

instead of the department stores to purchase gifts. In fact, we only received three complete place settings of fine china. On our seventh anniversary, we toured the wine county of Temecula, California, and at dinner that night, my husband hauled in a heavy box and set it in the center of our table. When I opened it, I found seven more of our Hancock place settings in the Lenox collection. The waiter walked by, amused and waiting until I finished. To his surprise, my husband insisted our meal be served on the new plates. Hesitant at first, concerned about breaking the new gifts, he finally agreed. What a wonderful surprise and lifelong gift from my husband.

Birth of a child: **My husband celebrates the life we brought into this world—our daughter—and on her birthday every year he buys me a gift, too. This makes me feel very loved and appreciated.**

On your next anniversary, deviate from what is expected when shopping for an anniversary gift. At any Hallmark store, ask for their free annual pocket calendar, which includes the suggested traditional and modern anniversary gift categories. You just might want to interpret the first year's modern of suggestion "clocks" as an excuse to travel to Switzerland, where the makers of the most accurate timepieces reside. The modern suggestion for year eight of linens/lace might whisk you and yours off to Ireland to touch the detailed creations in person. Don't forget to kiss the Blarney Stone for good luck while you are there. Or perhaps you two will opt to stay close to home but enroll together in a pottery class, honoring the traditional option earmarked appropriate for this anniversary.

TGIF

Make every Friday a reason for a private party for two, just because it is the last day of the work week. Fill a basket or serving tray with special treats for the both of you. If you include most of these essential ingredients in your romantic evening, it will be sure to prove an evening for love:

Aromatherapy: Lightly mist the room with the essence of sandalwood or frankincense. You could also release the heavenly aromas with an electronic or ceramic diffuser or in a bowl of hot water. Test different incense and scented candles.

Ambience: Create a cozy place to curl up together: outside on a picnic blanket with pillows, on the porch swing with a huge blanket, the hammock, or inside on the couch wearing your pajamas.

Music: Play romantic music in the background such as the album *The Peter Malick Group Featuring Norah Jones.*

Nibble Food: Lay out a small spread of finger food, especially aphrodisiacs like chocolate, roasted almonds, steamed artichokes—anything that does not require a lot of preparation is best.

Activity: Set up something you can do together: read words of poetry to each other, play your favorite board game, page through a photo album of yesteryear's memories, or write down your dreams of trips to take together in this lifetime.

> **Love is life. And if you miss love, you miss life.**
> —*Leo Buscaglia (1924–1998)*

Love Flowers: The word *tulip* is derived from the Turkish word *turban*, *tëlbent*. In Persia, if your beau gives you a red tulip, he is declaring his love. The black center represents his heart, burnt to a coal by love's passion.

chapter 9

home
SWEET HOME

*celebrate your life

> Feasting is also closely related to memory. We eat certain things in a particular way in order to remember who we are. Why else would you eat grits in Madison, New Jersey?
> —*Jeff Smith (b. 1939)*

From regional idiosyncrasies to All-American dishes—crayfish boils, potlucks, casseroles, and BBQs—everyone has their favorites that hold special memory and meaning.

Chocolate-chip cookies, tapioca pudding, rice crispy treats—foods that make us nostalgic for home or our childhood have a powerful pull over our senses. For my brother, the taste of strawberry shortcake, a thick biscuit piled high with juicy berries, immediately takes him home again to summers spent in rural Pennsylvania. Perfectly whipped potatoes

like Grandma used to make, or maybe Mom's chicken soup, meatloaf, or scalloped potatoes are the aromas and textures providing comfort the way our childhood home once
did—no matter where we are now.

Certain types of sandwiches instantly recall memories of childhood generally associated with
comfort. I remember the grilled cheese sandwiches oozing with white American cheese that my
mother made for my brother, sister, and me on rainy after-noons. Other times, it would be sandwiches with crunchy peanut butter and grape jam.

> The most remarkable thing about my mother is that for thirty years she served the family nothing but leftovers. The original meal has never been found.
>
> —*Calvin Trillin (b. 1935)*

Biscuits and gravy, nowadays considered a comfort food, was actually a meal of the poor. It was a plate of bread covered in gravy or sauce, which occasionally contained meat.

Comfort Foods

The one-dish wonders created lovingly by Mom bring back for-gotten memories of slower times and appreciative moments spent together as a family unit. Time was allowed to taste and savor the thoughtfully prepared dishes, rather than just "inhaling" fast-food the way too many of us do now.

A meal in a bowl, fixed in a wok, or served with rice, pasta, polenta, or salad as a base is comfort food for two reasons: one, it is easy to prepare, and two, it is easy to clean up (the two rules that I am most adamant about whenever I have to cook). Stews, soups, chili con carne, casseroles, stroganoff, goulash...you add to the list.

Memories of happier times return us more often than not to yesteryear with a simple bite of this or that. What is high on your list of comfort foods? Do you remember or recognize why you have this yearning? What memories are evoked? Treat yourself to a trip down memory lane. Make a list of your top ten comfort foods or regular cravings and then treat your family or friends.

These are also dinners that your beginner cooks can handle with ease. Let them loose this weekend on a test run. Hand them a bowl, the wok, the Crock-Pot, or clay pot.

Cravings

Once during my pregnancy I had a craving, not for pickles, but for scrambled eggs with diced ham and green peppers just like my mom used to make. I did not even like ham anymore, but off to the store I went to buy the necessary ingredients for an omelet for me and my baby. I had not had this combination of food in fifteen years, but there I was dicing, chopping, and frying at eight months pregnant.

Craving Chocolate

Chocolate, called the "food of the gods," is one of the world's most desired and romantic indulgences. Originally delivered to Europe by Spanish conquistadors, only the aristocrats could afford this extravagant beverage brought from the New World.

> **The Mason–Dixon Line is the dividing line between cold bread and hot biscuits.**
> —Bob Taylor (b. 1923)

> **So where did these cravings come from? I concluded it's the baby ordering in. Prenatal takeout. Even without ever being in a restaurant, fetuses develop remarkably discerning palates, and they are not shy about demanding what they want. If they get the hankering, they just pick up the umbilical cord and call. 'You know what would taste good right now? A cheeseburger, large fries, and a vanilla coke. And if you could, hurry it up, because I'm supposed to grow a lung in a half-hour.'**
> —Paul Reiser (b. 1957)

However, the chocolate drink consumed in great quantities (rumored to be up to fifty cups a day) by the Aztec emperor Montezuma bears little resemblance to what we eat today. The bitter, pungent drink called *cacahuatl* or *xocolatl* enjoyed by the Mayans and the Incas was doctored with sugar, vanilla, and cinnamon in Europe. In 1847, the English firm Fry & Sons created the first eating chocolate. Since the Swiss perfected the recipe in 1876, the world's appetite for chocolate seems insatiable.

Chocolate is indeed addictive to some and this discovery is hardly surprising. With a natural amphetamine that stimulates the central nervous system, eating milk, dark, or semisweet chocolate produces a feeling of well-being.

> **There are four basic food groups: milk chocolate, dark chocolate, white chocolate, and chocolate truffles.**
> —*Unknown*

At the beginning of the seventeenth century, chocolate houses became popular as meeting places to be seen and heard.

> **Strength is the capacity to break a chocolate bar into four pieces with your bare hands and then just eat one of the pieces.**
> —*Judith Viorst (b. 1931)*

Togetherness

Introduce a new idea into your everyday meals to bring the family together once again. Let food, and the preparation of it, be the common denominator between the ages. Simple togetherness activities, such as baking

South American Hot Cocoa: Hot chocolate is made by pouring boiling water into a cup, adding an ounce or so of a chocolate bar into the cup, and stirring until melted. Dip a slice of *pan de yema* (egg bread) into the thick and delicious beverage.

bread, making homemade raviolis, or going fishing for tonight's meal can be transformed into a mother-daughter, father-son, or regular Saturday tradition involving the entire family.

In Hershey, Pennsylvania, the streets are lined with lampposts that resemble a silver Hershey Kiss.

> **I have this theory that chocolate slows down the aging process...It may not be true, but do I dare take the chance?**
> —*Unknown*

There is something about warm homemade cookies and a glass of cold milk. The time spent sharing such a sweet treat with a child or baking cookies together will set the stage for comfort in your child's future. Teach your children (or partner) to bake. This special and perhaps messy time together will at least result in a batch of yummy cookies. And once they master this realm of the kitchen, step aside and let the little masters try their hands at breakfast. It is your duty to your future daughters-in-law to encourage cross-gender baking and cooking.

According to Nabisco, there are seventeen different animal shapes produced for menagerie crackers: bear, bison, camel, cougar, elephant, giraffe, gorilla, hippopotamus, hyena, kangaroo, lion, monkey, rhinoceros, seal, sheep, tiger, and zebra. Since they are packaged randomly, not all varieties make it into every box.

Initially it may be one big mess, but just think of all the additional time that you will have on your hands once you teach them.

Our everyday meals are just as important as our annual feasts. I recently attended a middle school graduation ceremony and want to share the poignant words from one of the speakers. As a high school guidance counselor for the last fifteen years, he made it a habit of asking seniors what advice they would give parents of freshman. Repeatedly they said, "We should have had dinner together more often."

> One cannot think well, love well, sleep well, if one has not dined well.
> —*Virginia Woolf (1882–1941)*

> Vegetables are a "must" on a diet. I suggest carrot cake, zucchini bread, and pumpkin pie.
> —*Garfield, in the cartoon Garfield created by Jim Davis (b. 1945)*

The Colorful Palate

Eat different colors every day. If you have toddlers at the table, make each meal a brilliant presentation of the rainbow and use this opportunity to teach them the names of the colors. Follow this advice and you will eat—naturally and easily—healthy. Besides, you will be teaching them valuable eating habits for a lifetime of good health. If you follow another food guide pyramid's recommendations other than the USDA's such as the Asian, Latin, Mediterranean, or the Vegetarian Diet Pyramid, your plate will automatically be loaded with freshness.

Medical studies have proven that the taste for fat developed during childhood is difficult to lose as an adult. Fast-food restaurants and prepackaged food manufacturers know of this battle many of us fight regularly and profit by targeting our preference with innumerable bad choices.

Rainbow of Health

Colorful fruits and vegetables, which provide essential nutrients and vitamins, improve your health and deliver needed energy in a low fat, natural package. Many fruits and vegetables are already packaged "to go," so add them to school lunches, picnics, tailgating parties, and care packages. Many also contain antioxidants that have been proven to slow age-related diseases.

Be sure to toss a few of these colorful ingredients into your party recipe. Your guests, your family and/or friends, will continue to benefit from your gesture long term:

Blue foods: Blueberries, eggplant, plums, blackberries, Marionberries, grapes, raspberries...

Helpful in the defense against harmful carcinogens, foods with a blue or purple tint are rich in vitamin C and high in fiber and potassium.

Passionate bites: strawberries, cherries, tomatoes, pink grapefruit, apples, beets, peppers, rhubarb, watermelon...

Red fruits add lycopene to your diet, a powerful antioxidant effective in reducing chances of various cancers.

Sunshine foods: corn on the cob, pineapple, pears, lemons, bananas, summer squash, wax beans, rutabaga, star fruit...

Yellow foods, rich in vitamin C, manganese, and the natural enzyme bromelain, which aides in digestion, are also high in fiber.

Good greens: chilies, green peppers, kiwi, lime, celery, spinach, collards, kale, broccoli, Brussels sprouts, asparagus, snow peas, green beans, lima beans, lettuce, pickles, cucumbers, artichoke...

Frankenstein Foods: Up to 70 percent of packaged foods—including soft drinks, ketchup, potato chips, cookies, ice cream, and cornflakes—contain products that have been genetically engineered. The Food and Drug Administration does not yet require labeling to identify if the food has Genetically Modified Organisms (GMOs) in its composition. Be safe and buy organic—certified organic foods do not contain GMOs.

Blueberries contain compounds called *anthocyanins*, which may help improve memory. Test this theory this morning and order a short stack of blueberry pancakes or a muffin...

The key cell-building nutrient found in leafy green vegetables, called folicate, protects your eyes and keeps the retina strong.

White foods: cauliflower, turnips, potatoes, onions, garlic, shallots...

White foods may help reduce the risk of cancerous tumors.

Orange treats: sweet potatoes, mangos, carrots, apricots, tangerines...

These orange treats from nature contain beta-carotene, an antioxidant that enhances the immune system, and are rich in vitamins B, C, and E, which help prevent birth defects.

A recent study by Ohio State University suggests black raspberries are almost 40 percent richer in antioxidants than blueberries and strawberries and may stop colon cancer.

Backyard Barbeque Bashes

The word *barbeque* is thought to have originated from the Haitian word *barbacoa*, which means "grill." Others speculate that its origin is French due to the phrase *de la barbe à la queue,* or in English that is "from the beard to the tail," indicative of the manner in which many meats and fish were grilled.

According to the Japanese, using a *hibachi,* or table barbecue, is a great way to barbecue. Many Americans have adopted this smaller scale version for dining outside, especially when tailgating.

Food tastes best when grilled over a wood-burning fire—better than over a gas grill and much better than charcoal. Work together to make dinner not only tasty but a special time together. Serve up hot beef skewers served over a premade vegetable and rice bowl.

Whatever you are grilling together, make sure it becomes a regular tradition—a party, of course. No stress, no pressure—just the opportunity to explore your creative side, side by side with those who count in your world. Teach your sons and daughters, too, to grill. No reason to have only one barbeque chef in the household.

Grilled Desserts

"In Asian and Mediterranean cuisines, cooking fruits and vegetables is an art form," says New York University's Marion Nestle. This is probably why vegetable dishes and grilled fruit desserts are plentiful on the menus in those restaurants.

For your husband's birthday or the holidays, consider giving him Su-Mei Yu's *Asian Grilling: 85 Satay, Kebabs, Skewers and Other Asian-Inspired Recipes for Your Barbeque.*

No-Fail Grilled Vegetables:

Potatoes: Scrub clean, quarter, rub with olive oil, and sprinkle with salt and pepper.

Sweet potatoes: Cut in half, brush with grapeseed oil or butter, sprinkle with nutmeg.

Squash: Slice, dab with sesame oil or butter, and sprinkle with parsley, oregano, or dill.

Tomatoes: Add cherry tomatoes to a kebab, or grill thick beefy slices of garden-grown varieties in a grilling basket or pan.

Mushrooms and Peppers: Grill separately or as an ingredient of a *satay*.

After dinner, do not let the fire die. For dessert tonight, try peaches, pineapple, pears, or mangos over the grill. Prior to cooking your dessert, use a steel brush to remove traces of the main entrée. Gently cook on both sides, and after removing from the fire, add just a pinch of brown sugar, maple syrup, or a sprinkle of ground cinnamon, nutmeg, or ginger. Drizzle with a bit of sweetened coconut milk or dot with a dab of fresh whipped cream. The combinations are endless, and each bite, luscious.

Spice Explorations

Your home sweet home does not have to be All-American—spice up your plate and parties a bit more. I invite you to open your spice cabinet and peer into the dark crevices. How often do you find yourself, or the chef of the house, using the same old couple of spices? In your exploration, you may discover many of the common herbs and spices used in the United States actually have faraway origins.

Throughout Asian, Arabic, and Mediterranean countries, spices were valued as much as gold and influenced many distinct dishes. Why not let old-time recipes from other cultures dictate your menu this evening? The local library or simpler yet, the Internet, can provide recipes and a four-color picture of the proposed dish all based around one spice. Cookbooks focusing on foreign and inventive spice recipes abound, so check one out for your next party.

Indian curries and *masalas* and African *tabils* and *harissas* plus good-ol' American barbeque and fish seasonings can all be a reason to throw a backyard bash and the rally to bring good friends together in the name of mixing. From Africa, India, and China, make your next feast an international collaboration of efforts. Ask each guest to bring a revered spice from antiquity and something to grill, and spend time in the kitchen mixing up taste-bud-awakening delights.

Spicy Lies

The expression "you get what you pay for" is especially true where spices are concerned. Always read the label—even if your purchase appears to be just a

---

Good-bye Salt! Hello Spices!

Meats: thyme, sage, cracked black or white pepper, yellow, white, or purple onions, garlic, nutmeg, marjoram, or bay leaf

Poultry: ginger, oregano, paprika, rosemary, tarragon, sage, or thyme

Fish: aïoli, fresh lemon or lime juice, curry powder, marjoram, dry mustard, dill, paprika, or salsa of any flavor—peach, mango, or roasted garlic

---

Spice Storage: Dried whole spices stored in airtight containers in a cool, dry cupboard will keep up to a year. Within a few months, ground spices fade in color and taste. Let your sense of smell be your guide for whether to keep or toss the spices in your cupboard.

bottle of vanilla or chili powder. You might think that you are buying the real thing, but closer scrutiny is the only way to be sure.

McCormick Pure Vanilla Extract contains vanilla bean extractives in water, 35 percent alcohol, and corn syrup.

To find pure vanilla, shop for vanilla pods or vanilla beans available in health food, specialty food, or gourmet grocery stores. The price tag is quite a bit higher, but since you are buying the real thing, you can use less of it than the artificial version.

To those living in the Southwest, chili powder means ground pure chiles and nothing else. What is offered in most grocery stores nationwide is chili powder with a blend of other spices. Chili powder is commonly a mixture of ground chiles, cumin, oregano, salt, silicon dioxide (free flowing agent), and garlic. Unless the ingredient label reads "100 percent chili powder," it is usually not pure. Looking for the real stuff with a kick? Try a specialty store or shop online.

Cassia, or Chinese cinnamon, is one of the oldest spices, recorded as early as 2700 BC and mentioned in the Bible (Exodus 30:23–25). In the United States, cassia is sold as cinnamon, whereas in Great Britain, the two spices are differentiated.

Who would have guessed that the spice chili could affect so many diverse dishes? This week, try pungent Chinese chili oil or a dash of the red powder of paprika—essential in goulash and other Hungarian specialties, and widely used in Spain.

Throughout the Deep South, this red pepper seasons meals. Beside the bottles of mustard and ketchup lined up at the diner counter, expect to see a red or green bottle of Tabasco sauce, too. To shake up things at home, add a bottle to your refrigerator shelf.

Hot Tip: To cut the blaze of my spicy Southwestern recipes, I stir up a huge pitcher of freshly squeezed lemonade. It truly hits the spot—or should I say "puts out the fire"?

Sample the golden hot pepper sauce served as a condiment with dishes in the West Indies. In Indonesia, a spicy hot pepper relish, or *sambal,* is served in small dishes as an accompaniment to foods. For your next party, go shopping for this hot condiment.

Tonight's meal could have its origin from a Malaysian recipe and be served with a red-hot chili sauce made sweet with the addition of ginger.

Invite new spice blends into your kitchen. Stir up the bubbling pot on the stove with a French *quatre-epices* mixture, or "four spices," a mix of seasonings based on pepper and used in dishes that require simmering.

Be daring and pull out the mortar and pestle to grind your personal mix of Cajun seasoning: black pepper, cayenne, coarse sea salt, dried thyme, paprika, cumin, mustard powder, and dried oregano. Who knows where this evening meal will take you…but do go; the change will do you and your taste buds a world of good.

In Turkey, chili is a condiment.

Hot Spice: Ginger, fresh or dried, will kick up the taste of any dish. Allegedly, this is also a characteristic of redheaded women named Ginger; perhaps being christened with a fiery name results in a zeal for life and a hot temperament.

Follow the Spice Caravan

The Greek merchant sailor Hippalus discovered that if he sailed with the monsoon winds, he could lessen the amount of time it took to sail to India. Previously, the journey for spices took two years. Now in less than a year, the booty could be expected and Romans became extravagant with spices in their cooking,

About 1550 BC, the Ebers papyrus, an Egyptian medical document, recorded the common use of anise, caraway, cassia, cardamom, mustard, sesame, fenugreek, and saffron.

perfumes, cosmetics, and medicine.

The most expensive spice in the world is saffron, costing ten times as much as vanilla and fifty times as much as cardamom. The thread-like stigmas of the saffron crocus must be hand-picked and are so light that more than twenty thousand flowers yield only four ounces of the spice. Try the distinctive taste, color, and aroma of this pricey spice in the Spanish fish and rice dish of *paella*, Italian *risotto*, or a French *bouillabaisse*. You may find that this is one spice you must have.

Once long ago, I went home with my friend Sheila during college break and had my first—but not my last—taste of Iranian cooking in a huge platter of rice richly colored with turmeric and spotted with raisins and small meatballs.

Pepper, the most popular spice from the Orient, solely inspired the search for new and quicker routes to the East. Ginger and turmeric followed accordingly in popularity.

During the Middle Ages, pepper, the valued and expensive spice, was often used as currency for rents, dowries, and taxes.

On many islands in the Pacific, turmeric, a member of the ginger family, is worn as a protective charm to ward off evil spirits.

Herbal Counters

Basil, chives, dill, oregano, rosemary, sage, and thyme are all easy herbs to cultivate on your kitchen countertop. Trust me, the queen of black thumbs; even I can make these young shoots grow—at least long enough to collect a small harvest to freeze for the winter. I clip and pluck what I need while cooking and then gather the remaining herbs to store in the freezer. Simply mark the plastic bag with the expiration date (four months from the date of harvest) and enjoy fresh herbs whenever you want.

Invite your family to play in the dirt with you. Together, you can grow herbs and nurture quality time.

Fast Food

For those who find no joy in the *Joy of Cooking* and are looking to create healthy and fast food for their families, I recommend *Fast Appetizers* by Hugh Carpenter and Teri Sandison.

A great picture book for those culinarily challenged, these authors promise light meals in less than fifteen minutes. The first night that you serve this ideal meal, treat your small party to the movie *Mermaids* where Cher stars as the single mom who serves only appetizers for every meal. It may work once a week in your household and be a cause for celebration—a departure from the ordinary.

Bye-Bye Butter!
Following are suggestions for seasonings that render butter unnecessary for a richly flavorful and delicious dish.

Carrots: cinnamon, cloves, marjoram, nutmeg, rosemary, dill, or sage

Corn: cumin, curry powder, sliced onion, paprika, or parsley

Green beans: sliced roasted almonds, tarragon

Broccoli: fresh squeezed lemon

Details Count

Looking at the details of what makes a vacation home comfortable, we can apply these notions in our current abode and not wait until we finally secure our dream home or a second home.

We know what the comforts of a home should include. All we have to

Recycle: To dress the dining-room table tonight, cut a single flower stem and place it in an unusual container. My favorite recycled "vases" are colored glass bottles and uniquely shaped jars from imported oils and jellies. Tie the neck with raffia or a ribbon; add marbles, pebbles, or seashells in the bottom of the vase.

do is take inventory of what we are dreaming of. What did our childhood or grandparents' houses give us? Both lists will include warmth, comfort, and safety. This is what it means to come home again. Create these experiences in your home.

With an appreciation of both simple, pure foods and the finer niceties in life, you can include them in everyday living and create moments beyond just eating dinner again for the sixth time this week. Apply the conviction "any reason for a feast," and focus on the experience to have a healthy and fulfilling time any night of the week at home.

Feng Shui consultant Sally Fretwell says, "The kitchen is the nucleus of the house. Ideally, you want to feel uplifted in the kitchen."

> **Show me another pleasure like dinner, which comes every day and lasts an hour.**
> —*Charles Maurice de Talleyrand-Périgord (1754–1838)*

What We Eat Equals Who We Are

Home is where we should be able to find our balance, a sanctuary where rejuvenation and tranquility can be easily found. When we are in balance with nature and ourselves, we experience vibrant health and energy; however, whenever we are out of balance, we become more susceptible to outside stressors, which can lead to illness and unhappiness.

Ayurvedic medicine, *"ayu,"* which means "life," and *"veda,"* which means "the knowledge," has been practiced in India for more than five

Kitchen Karma:
- Trade traditional fluorescent lighting for full-spectrum fluorescent, which emits a more natural light, or choose task lighting, chandeliers, or position counter lamps to soften the mood.
- Change the ambiance with warm and inviting colors: calming earth tones or accents with spicy red or soothing cobalt blue.
- Turn off the television and play relaxing music.
- Reduce clutter on the countertops.
- Create a comfy place to sit.

thousand years, and places an equal emphasis on the individual's body, mind, and spirit to restore harmony within. This alternative and preventive medicine combines natural therapies such as dietary changes, exercises, yoga, meditation, massage, and herbal tonics and sweat baths as a highly personalized approach to maintaining health.

By exploring *Ayurvedic* cuisine, you can change how you feel by what you eat. The main principle of this type of cooking is to eat what is best suited for your *dosha,* or your metabolic body type. The *Ayurvedic* body type is similar to the Western view of body types: thin, muscular, or heavyset.

Review the following *Ayurvedic* body type list to identify your primary *dosha*:

	Vata	*Pitta*	*Kapha*
Body	Thin	Medium build	Heavyset
Skin	Cool, dry	Warm, ruddy, perspiring	Cool, thick, pale, oily
Eating	No schedule	Does not miss a meal	Eats slowly
Sleep	No schedule	Regular bedtime, eight hours	Sleeps long, heavily
Nature	Enthusiastic	Intelligent, articulate	Tolerant, forgiving
Personality	Imaginative	Orderly, efficient	Graceful, relaxed
Temperament	Vivacious	Intense, passionate	Affectionate
Work Ethics	Hyperactive	Short temper, perfectionist	Procrastination
Ailments	Anxiety, nervous disorders	Ulcers, heartburn	Obesity, allergies
Illnesses	Constipation, cramps	Hemorrhoids, acne	High cholesterol

Each body types flourishes under a specific diet, exercise program, and lifestyle—changes that can be made easily in the comfort of home.

We are primarily comprised of one body type but can have a mixture of others. The five elements found in nature are also found within us: ether/space, air, fire, water, and earth. Traditional Chinese medicine also recognizes these elements in their medical treatments.

The three metabolic body types, or *doshas*, are: *vata* (ether/space and air), *pitta* (fire and water), and *kapha* (water and earth). Imbalances in one's *dosha* can affect mental and physical health. Strive in your home comforts, diet, and personal and career life to be balanced and work to correct any imbalances.

Once you recognize your *dosha*, consult the many cookbooks now available to determine what food types will best fuel your mind, body, and spirit. Attending seminars about this new way of living may be in your best interest, too. When you feel off-balance you can then apply the antidote to regain your center.

You may very well see that the old American cliché "you are what you eat" holds true in the *Ayurvedic* way of living well—or not so well, depending on what you do indeed consume.

> *Reuse:* At the holidays, arrange a small sampling of your cherished holiday ornaments as a centerpiece. Use a rich, velvety fabric to showcase them or place them on a silver platter covered with pine boughs.

Home Sweet Home

Our home is our castle, our sanctuary, and our safe place in the world. It's where we can go for encouragement, rest, and nourishment. Yet many Americans dream of having a second home, a special place where they can go to recharge, be comfortable, and spend time outdoors either alone or in good company.

I say why not make your primary residence your dream home today? Spend the next three-day holiday weekend at home and do everything that you would do if on vacation:

no cleaning or cooking—and if you must, only as a group effort—no stress and no clocks. In fact, turn off the phone and let the answering machine do its job. You can check on it occasionally, but do not let any ringer (cell phones and pagers, too) interrupt this tranquil time. Celebrate your life at home.

Make your home a special place, overflowing with comfort and tranquility. If even just a corner of a room or the front or back porch, find a spot within your house to truly relax where no worries can find you. Do not allow problems to follow you here.

Lock the door, turn on the music, or simply revel in the pure silence of your space and time. Make this second home a possibility now, and within walking distance. It will be the best decision you will make all year. Now, whenever you want to go on vacation, all you have to do is go across the house.

Like our European and Australian sisters who go away on "holiday" every August, you too can travel annually to anywhere that you want to go. Simply, create a "holiday" at home with any of these decorating ideas and visit alpine resorts, Pacific isles, exotic Asian destinations, Parisian cafés, or Italian *terrazzo* without leaving home and spending a fortune.

If a nautical destination is your preferred dream vacation, then decorate the guest bath and retreat to this serene water environment

Reduce: Go through your pantry and cupboards. Exactly how many coffee cups does your household need? The same goes for the excess in pots and pans or bakeware. Reduce your kitchen inventory to what is essential and cooking will become even easier without having to dig and unearth. Donate the extra items to charity.

Renew: Give new life to old dishes by mix and matching. Use wine glasses for water glasses, use the fine china for salad and dessert dishes with the everyday dishes, or serve pudding in a teacup.

whenever your spirits need a boost. Subscribe to *Coastal Living* magazine and lose yourself among the picturesque beach cottages and long stretches of white sand beaches.

With bamboo blinds, a few tropical plants, a coconut-scented candle, and a fountain, set up your peaceful corner of the world to remind you to return or tempt you to visit a South Pacific island someday.

If the mountains move you, then redecorate the library or living room with a rustic cabin motif. Hang vintage skiing posters from the fifties alongside a pair of antique wooden skis and snowshoes on the walls. For a moment of downtime in the middle of a busy week, light a pine-scented candle and cuddle under a wool plaid blanket with a cup of hot chocolate.

This weekend design your vacation spot at home, and for peace of mind—visit frequently. Be creative and recreate whatever environment your spirit is craving. Escape here whenever you can and watch what this magical retreat can do for your mind, body, and spirit. Now when your upcoming vacation is months away, you can still have a "holiday"—no matter what your calendar says.

chapter 10

parties
MADE EASY

* ### smashing successes

> ## The ornament of a house is the friends who frequent it.
> —*Ralph Waldo Emerson (1803–1882)*

Legend reports that Dom Pérignon exclaimed, "Come quickly; I am tasting the stars!" upon his discovery of champagne. Our celebrations of life can bring us a similar enthusiasm and delight.

For some people, every day is a reason to throw an impromptu party. For others, due to busyness or the lack of inclination or self-confidence about hosting a party, only the standard obligatory dates such as birthdays and official holidays are reserved for celebration.

From distant kitchens and international cafés and restaurants, I learned how to eat healthy food that tastes good and is easy to prepare and have brought this strategy into my menu planning for parties. The expression, "We eat with our eyes," is quite true, another lesson learned early in my party-planning days. While I have not been awarded the coveted *Merité Agricole* by the French Republic or honored as the "Culinarian of the Year" by the American Culinary Federation, I have discovered the importance of creating a warm and inviting environment and setting an attractive, self-service table so I do not have to be the waitress. As cookbook author Colin Cowie says, "Plan a party that won't keep you chained to the stove."

Team Approach

There is absolutely no reason to do it all by yourself. Take a team approach to the task of hosting a successful party—the one that

> Plumeria, the traditional flower of the Hawaiian lei, will always say, "Aloha."

all want to attend, but no one wants to plan, set up, cook for, and clean up afterwards. By dividing the labor and sharing in the excitement of the upcoming event, the anticipation alone will ensure the party throwers and the partygoers will have the best time.

Besides, it is the time together that means the most when the last dish is put away. Be sure to put the men and children on the task list to make them feel part of the party. Do not limit the men's inclusion to just taking out the garbage or barbequing. See where their secret skills truly lie. You may be pleasantly surprised.

Hired Help

If the thought of throwing a party sends you into an anxiety attack, my solution is simple. Hire a caterer, chef, cook, waiter, or behind-the-scenes helper, perhaps your niece and nephew, a high-school or college student, or your best friend who thrives on celebrations.

Ask for help.

I learned this lesson the hard way at my husband's birthday. I envisioned an Italian feast with lasagna and wanted to invite everyone, thinking only about half would come since it

Four Ways to Throw a Party:

From Scratch: select a casserole dish, one-dish dinner, or hearty soup or chili recipe. Or if you are a gourmet chef in residency, whip up a five-course meal and present it to your appreciative party of four.

To Go: Thai, BBQ ribs and chicken, Chinese, Mexican—all the offerings for an excellent gala are available. You can still theme it and rather than spending your time cooking, decorate and take a nap prior to party time.

Mix It Up: Prepare some foods from scratch; order other dishes from the local bakery or a restaurant.

Pot Luck: This year, my birthday fell in the middle of our kitchen remodeling. We called upon our culinarily-blessed guests to surprise us, and we were not disappointed.

Folklore claims that witches used parsley in their magic flying potion. This Halloween, float a sprig on top of chicken "bone" soup and watch the little ones really soar.

was Memorial Day weekend. Well, everyone came—all eighty people plus kids. In addition to cooking for a solid day and night prior to the party, I played waitress all night long at the feast.

Ask for help and keep it simple. Get everyone in the game. Ask people to bring a dish—their favorite, or one to match the theme of the party.

Julia Child I am not, but I have found ways to surprise people with simple yet creative dishes and fun party ideas. From a murder-mystery party or a wine-and-cheese-tasting get-together with close friends to a wild Halloween party for the neighborhood kids where our garage is transformed into a spooky alley: all it takes is a simple idea and a few friends to help pull it all together. Sometimes, I assign guests a job or a task as they arrive in order to make them a part of the party from the first minute. They have fun, and I get the set of extra hands needed to make the party a success.

Party Props

If this party that you have in mind is simply for your family but requires a bit of prep work and finishing niceties, enlist each and every member to assist with the creation of a lavish, yet well-worth-the-time meal. Make the preparation a party, too.

Pass out whimsical aprons or crisp white ones, real chef's hats or paper ones purchased at a restaurant supply store, and of course, you must assign titles to those elected to assist. Make them on the computer and print them out on white mailing-label stickers. You might need a *sous* chef, definitely a master chef, perhaps a pastry chef for dessert, a trusting and does-not-sink-under-pressure line cook, prep chef, and lastly, the *garde-manger* or food decorator. Add a hostess to set a handsome table and a waiter, or several, may come in handy if you still need and have the extra hands. Assign and rotate the duties of bus boy, dishwasher, and waiter from time to time at these everyday home-based celebrations.

This type of family cooperation also works best when everyone is in town for the holidays. Why should one or two people be stuck in the kitchen when the rest of the crowd is enjoying appetizers in the fading hours of the day?

Once the members of your household see the making of the mouth-watering food, there will be a greater appreciation of future meals and desserts—which may previously have been thought to magically appear on their plates. From behind the pleasant sounds of chopping, stirring, dicing, and thudding of dough, the evening air will be filled with the astonishment of "Look what I did!" You may be surprised at the willingness to try, and let them be surprised as well with their hidden talents.

Keys to Success

Every party can be a success with a few key ingredients:

1. *Planning*: A little bit of foresight as to what the event should be about, whom to invite, and what foods to serve allows for the theme of the event to be the glue—intermingling all together from start to end.

2. *Originality*: It has been said that there are no new ideas, be it in Hollywood movies, the latest released novels, or your best friend's wedding, yet the creative personality always finds a new way. Originality is simply taking an old idea and twisting it, adding something else to it, or taking something away. The merging, blending, and recreating makes an old idea new again. Try this approach with your next bash.

3. *Courage*: Once you step in the direction of throwing a party with a new spin, do not back out. Announce the theme to all as soon as you can to allow them ample time to buy into the concept. If your guests come prepared to participate, it will be a successful party.

Borrow Ideas

Want to deviate from the typical American cuisine for your next party? Do not go it alone. Every bookstore, not to mention every pubic library, has well-stocked shelves of sacred scriptures—cookbooks,

Creative Substitutions:

- For an international party and menu, use a map of the world for a tablecloth.
- When hosting an afternoon tea, complete with crumpets, lemon curds, and other dainty finger foods, substitute paper doilies for place mats.
- If hosting a tailgating party inside for the Super Bowl, line the serving tables with AstroTurf.
- Hosting a pajama party for a young girl's birthday? Use pillowcases for place mats, and place slippers on the chairs as party favors.
- At your next sushi dinner party, use bamboo sushi mats for the table runner and fill a glass vase with uncooked long-grain jasmine rice. Stick the chopsticks into the rice so your guests can choose the pair they would like to use.
- At a Western barbeque, dress the table in denim fabric and accent with red-and-blue bandanas.

with sales exceeded only by the Bible. Visit the culinary aisles and go home with a professional whose voice will help you maneuver the trappings and treats of international dishes.

Borrow ideas from your favorite restaurant. If you like the manner in which the table is set: all white or splashed with bold colors, pillar candles tied with sheer organza ribbons or wrapped with live ivy, or the way the restaurant is lit by tiny, clear glass bulbs strung around its ceiling or the simple fold of the cloth napkins, take these ideas home with you. Carry a small pad of paper to capture the idea or sketch the concept.

> *Easy Centerpieces:* Fill a glass vase or decorative bowl
> a third full with cranberries, acorns, or walnuts.

To feature color in your celebration, use fruit in a decorative bowl. For Sunday brunch, use a glass bowl of oranges as your centerpiece. At your Hawaiian luau, fill a wooden bowl with papayas, mangos, limes and lemons, or coconuts. Hosting a backyard barbeque bash? Place apple crates with shiny Granny Smith, Macintosh, and Jonathan apples on each of the tables to hold down the tablecloth.

> *Amuse-bouche* are what *hors d'oeuvres* were to America in the 1950s, now standard fare at French dinner parties.

Easy Starters

Tapas, hors d'oeuvres, zakuski, appetizers— whatever you call the prelude to a meal, this small tray of tasty bites is meant to be just that. Remember to keep the finger food bite-sized so that conversation can continue and one hand is free for handshakes or a beverage.

Since *hors d'oeuvres* are not the main meal, simply offer a taste of what is to come and present no more than three appetizers. Somehow over the decades, the serving size of appetizers has grown, too. Now, when dinner is served, we are already full. Limit servings to three pieces per person. Serve with toothpicks to minimize clean up. If serving appetizers as the main meal, serve three to six varieties with three to five pieces per person.

The French gathered for an aperitif before dinner to "whet the appetite."

The Spanish word *tapas* means "cover" or "lid." The custom started in the *bodegas* (wineries) when the sherry maker would place little morsels of food—a few olives, a slice of ham or homemade sausage—on a small lid and balance it on top of the glass. Competition began between the local taverns to see who served the best *tapas*.

Mezes are traditional Mediterranean appetizers—trays and dishes of rustic breads, olives, pickled vegetables, goat cheese, crackers, and *tapenade* (olive paste).

Tapenade Recipe:
1¾ cup pitted Kalamata olives
1 clove garlic, chopped
2 tbsp. capers
1 tsp. chopped fresh thyme
1 tsp. chopped fresh rosemary
3 tbsp. lemon juice
4 tbsp. olive oil
Purée all but the olive oil in a blender; gradually add the olive oil into the mixture until a paste is formed. Serve on country bread.

Numbers Count

Many hostesses fret over the perfect number of guests to invite. Antiquity reveals the magical process of how many guests to invite; feel free to borrow from their superstitions. For example, an early Roman dinner was typically three or nine—as many as the Graces, but no more than the Muses. Under Emperor Augustus, when women were beginning to take their place in Roman society, twelve men and

In Hawaii, *pupu* is the Hawaiian term assigned to appetizers.

Easy Appetizer: Roasted Elephant Garlic
    1 head of elephant garlic (or 4 of regular)
    3 tbsp. olive oil
Slice off the top of the head of garlic and drizzle with olive oil. For additional flavor, sprinkle with rosemary, thyme, or sage, and place in a garlic baker with a lid. (A pie tin covered in foil can also be used.) Bake at 400° Fahrenheit for thirty minutes. Serve hot on toasted baguette slices, spread like butter.

twelve women would be invited to honor the twelve gods and goddesses.

Over in neighboring Greece, to show respect to Pallas, the goddess of wisdom, and as a symbol of her virginity, the host and hostess would choose the sterile number seven for the number of guests. Yet the Greeks sometimes preferred the number six, since it was a round number.

Superstitions still hold firmly in France where any number of dinner guests except thirteen is acceptable.

In my household, this number is purely arbitrary in that it is whoever says "yes." If we run out of dishes, we use paper; if there are not enough chairs, we recline like the Romans and Greeks on outdoor patio furniture, in the hammocks, or on the lawn.

In the simplest terms, a party—any get-together—is a celebration of life, a prized opportunity to share

Floral Options: Match your party's ambiance to any of these perfect flowers: Queen Anne's lace, tulips, ranunculus, daffodils, gardenias, pansies, nasturtiums, violets, or sweet peas.

Easy Centerpiece: Do as the Mennonites do and set the table with a cake stand and a proud cake as the centerpiece.

in good food and good times with those closest to us, those who make life special as well as those new to us, who may introduce original ideas.

Fast Decorating Ideas

My favorite part of planning a party is to go through my house and improvise with what I already have. You will be surprised at what presents itself if you look around with fresh eyes. Can't see any new arrangements or combinations? Call a friend. She will help you find new treasures, perfect centerpieces, buffet accents, or lawn decorations.

Nature's Alternatives: **If you only have time to shop in nature, arrange attractive leaves such as ivy, geranium, or magnolia in a beautiful vase or add a few small branches from a golden aspen, autumn-tinged maple, or an evergreen tree. Mist the arrangement with a water bottle to give the plants a rain-kissed fresh look.**

Table Beauty
Use any of the following to add interest to your dining or buffet table:
- Pebbles
- Seashells
- Wreaths
- Garden urns
- Topiaries
- Tabletop statues
- Leather-bound books
- Glass figurines
- Antique teaspoons
- International coins
- Gold-foil candies
- Three-tiered fruit trays
- Driftwood

The Essential Party Kitchen List
Keep these on hand, and you can make it a party at a moment's notice:
- Paper Japanese umbrellas
- Plastic coconut drink shells
- Ice buckets
- Metal containers, wash buckets, beach buckets to hold iced drinks
- Colorful sarongs
- Votive candles
- Holiday white lights or other decorative lighting sets

One secret of many busy women when hosting a party is to pare down the ingredient list. Keep food preparation simple so that the true flavors can be tasted. Enhance top-quality ingredients with fresh organic fruit and herbs, excellent chocolate, or aromatic spices, and savor the pure fragrances and tastes.

At Home with Friends

The best times are those spent with friends who are relaxed in your home, no matter its current state. Your truest friends are those who will dine with you on the front porch while your kitchen is being remodeled, even if dinner is just a frozen pizza. Find these people and invite them over often. These are the parties that count the most in life, the simple ones with people who care.

For intimate dinners or small groups, cluster similar-shaped items:
- Place three different kinds of bread-sticks in pint beer glasses.
- Light taper candles in empty wine bottles.
- Pour salted nuts into shallow bowls.

Spontaneous Celebrations

Sometimes parties just happen. Out at the ball field when the game ends and before you want to stop having fun, why not invite the crowd over to your backyard? Never miss an opportunity to be in the presence of good people and good conversation. Be prepared and this little *fête* will be easy. Delegate the courses of the menu on the spot so everyone can stop at home or the store and arrive with the party goods. If your picnic basket is already

Different Twists on Party Regulars:
- Serve *café au lait* the traditional way—in bowls—as they do in France.
- Mix mimosas with fresh-squeezed tangerine juice instead of orange juice.
- Host a tea-tasting party starting with black, oolong, green, and proceeding to white, red, and herbal.

packed and waiting for the next outing, you will be ready, too, at home when the doorbell rings.

Party Favors

Why do kids get to have all the fun? As adults, we generally are reserved and neither participate in party games nor go home with party favors. This must change. Bring out the piñatas, pass around the party favors, and play games once again.

Arrange any of these party favors on the dining-room table and give the small token of your appreciation to your guests as they depart:

· Small potted pansies with a colorful taper candle in the center.
· Potted kitchen herbs: rosemary, lavender, basil, thyme, oregano, or lemon balm.
· Take Polaroid photos of the guests and insert into a magnetic picture frame.
· Holiday Dinners: Place a different Santa Claus ornament at each place setting.
· Baby Showers: Arrange angel statues in the center of the table.
· Girl-to-Woman Celebrations: Give each guest miniature books filled with inspirational quotes.

Ideas for Outdoor Garden Parties: Brunch or Nighttime Soirées
- Add pillows and blankets to the patio furniture.
- Spread picnic blankets on the lawn (put a tarp down first to stop the dew).
- Create ambient lighting with tiki torches, hot-chili-pepper lights or other food-shaped lights, or hang metal or paper lanterns in the trees.

Easy Party Favors: Use small terra-cotta pots wrapped with colorful cloth napkins to give to friends for their patio gardens.

Barbara Sipos of Westminster, Colorado, suggests making floral pens to give as party favors. Wrap pens with green floral tape and secure a fabric flower at the top.

Permission to Shop

While traveling around our beautiful country on one of your exploratory trips, tasting new regional foods or discovering a new recipe, be sure to shop for mementos of your vacation and bring home party favors for your next gala.

This habit of shopping with a "party eye" will bring happiness to you two-fold. Your treasure will be a remembrance of past good times and an insurance of good times to come. Anything you find in red, white, or blue will fit nicely with a patriotic-themed occasion. Holiday items are always a sure thing for seasonal celebrations and usually on sale in the off-season.

Music is always a great addition to your party favor supply cabinet. Let your guests travel the world through the international lyrics and upbeat tempo played at your festivals.

Invitations

As with almost any event, much of the joy can be found in the anticipation of the occasion. These days, people are extremely busy. Try to give them as much notice as possible and offer babysitting options if you have children, too. At our

> Renee Maurer of Lakewood, Colorado, uses *www.evite.com* to customize invitations, enter a guest list, and keep track of the RSVPs.

parties, we normally let all the kids camp at one house up the street and hire as many sitters as necessary.

For your next batch of party invitations, try iron-on transfers or fabric paints on cloth napkins, a pillowcase for a slumber party, or a bandana for a Western barbeque. If the number invited is large, visit the local T-shirt screener.

> The essential oil of grapefruit, Melissa, or mandarin orange or the spices of cardamom, coriander, ginger, and black pepper can stimulate conversation.

Party Aromatherapy

Wonderful scents are key in creating a welcoming ambiance. Set a pot of water to boil, add two or three cinnamon sticks or vanilla pods, or a handful of whole cloves. Reduce the fragrant mixture to a simmer—perfect for early-in-the-day get-togethers.

For events later in the day or evening, simmer fresh or dried basil leaves over a low boil to infuse the party air with expectation of savory delights. Before the guests arrive, place a few small bowls in key areas with some of the fragrant herb to identify the source of this alluring scent.

More Great Party Ideas

Here are some themes you might want to try out for yourself and your friends and family.

The Processed-Food Party

Darcy Henderson of Portland, Oregon

Since all of Darcy's friends and siblings were following some sort of rather strict diet—vegetarian, raw food, detox, or yogic—they occasionally bemoaned the fact that they didn't get to eat the comfort foods of their childhood: green-bean casserole made with canned soup and crunchy onions, mashed sweet potatoes topped with marshmallows, pigs in a blanket, etc.

The invitations to this wild bash asked each guest to bring something edible containing three or more processed-food ingredients. Favorites included: Twinkies tiramisu, Spam sushi, and Pineapple-Melon Jello rings. Prizes were awarded for most creative new dish and for categories of best appetizer, salad, main dish, and dessert.

Guests came dressed as Betty Crocker look-alikes, the BBQ man, and campy '50s couples in an attempt to win the coveted best-costume prize. The party was made more outrageous with the addition of croquet, Twister, and late-night polka dancing. The processed-food party, hosted the first time on a whim, is now an annual and much-anticipated event in Portland.

Progressive Dinner Parties

When our friends and we were the parents of toddlers, we infrequently dined out at fancy restaurants. Sitters were hard to come by, and there was the cost factor and the fact that most of us were just too tired to go out after a full week of work either at home with the young ones or at the office. One Saturday after bemoaning this reality with a neighbor, we decided to make our own trendy restaurant, and the idea of hosting a progressive-dinner party was born.

> **The road to a friend's house is never long.**
> —Danish proverb

I invite you to do the same. Hire one brave baby-sitter (or maybe two), put all the kids at one house, and then go to the other "restaurants" for appetizers, salad and bread, the main course, and dessert.

Make it a tradition to do this once in the summer, then try it in the winter, and maybe decide to host a progressive-dinner party every time the seasons change. You get to see friends who desperately crave adult conversation, and eat great food with minimal preparation. You might even manage to squeeze in an evening stroll with your significant other.

Here Come the Bridesmaids: Joyce Abariotes of Wahoo, Nebraska, hosts an annual Bad Bridesmaid's Dress Contest. About forty-five women show up in their ugliest dresses, some not worn in almost three decades.

Easter Party

For the adventurous party planner, here is an idea to liven up any Easter Sunday spread: use real sod on the Easter table instead of a tablecloth. The best setting for this event is probably outside on the patio or the lawn. First cover the table with a tarp or plastic, then the pieces of sod. Decorate your grassy table with flowers or Easter eggs. Later, after the guests have gone home, you can simply pick up your "green" tablecloth and place the sod where it is needed on the lawn.

Hire someone (or assign a family member) to dress up as the Easter Bunny and shower the kids with plastic eggs filled with chocolate and coins. Make sure that you have a camera ready to capture these priceless memories. Party stores should have a few costumes for rent, but call at least three months in advance to reserve. If you are good with a sewing machine, so much the better, or if you know someone who is, hire her to make your bunny costume.

Arabian Nights

Transform your living room into a relaxing Middle Eastern tent. Drape your living room walls in swaths of rich regal fabric and line the floor and couches with equally elegant pillows of all shapes and sizes. Play the black-and-white movie of *Lawrence of Arabia* with the sound muted and let it run in the background of the party.

Upon arrival, direct your guests to their separate changing rooms. Rent camel-herder costumes for the men and belly-dancing costumes for the women. You might want to purchase a belly-dancing instructional video or hire a professional to show the group a few moves. Provide *zills,* or finger cymbals, and hip scarves as party favors to those who wish to master the art of belly dancing.

For a fast and tasty appetizer, head to the closest deli and pick up ready-made containers of tabbouleh and hummus. Tabbouleh is a refreshing Middle Eastern salad made from bulgar (cracked wheat), tomato, parsley or fresh mint, olive oil, lemon juice, and seasoning such as ground cinnamon or allspice. Serve with toasted pita bread cut into triangles or leaves of Belgian endive or white cabbage to use as a scoop.

Hummus, made from crushed chickpeas, comes in a variety of flavors from roasted garlic to eggplant and spicy three-pepper. Serve

Sundaes on Any Day: In the neighborhood, take turns hosting a good, old-fashioned ice-cream social. Ask each neighbor to bring a different topping. Think how great this summertime treat will taste if you make your favorite flavors.

instead of ranch dressing on your vegetable tray.

Baba ghanoush is a Middle Eastern puree of eggplant, tahini (sesame paste), olive oil, lemon juice, and garlic. Use it as a spread or a dip for pita bread or flat bread.

Just Desserts

Many foods found in the American diet, as well as those adopted from intercontinental menus, not only have strange names, but have equally bizarre origins.

Baked Alaska, the distinctive and delicate dessert of ice cream encased in meringue, was created by a chef at the famous New York restaurant Delmonico's to mark the United States's purchase of Alaska in 1869. Supposedly, Baked Alaska was brought back into vogue at the Hôtel de Paris in Monte Carlo, with credit going to Chef Jean Giroix.

If you have never tasted this spectacular dessert or if it has been years since the last time, start looking for an approaching milestone in your life (or someone else's) to order it. This is one dessert special enough to mark any

Tropical Isles: For a blast of tropical flavor, serve key lime sorbet in coconut shells. To drain the milk from the coconut, pierce the softest eye. Preheat the oven to 375° Fahrenheit and heat for five to ten minutes to make it easier to crack the coconut in half. Allow to cool, then scoop the sorbet with a large ice-cream scooper, drop it into the coconut shell half, and sprinkle with coconut shavings.

Different Flavors of Lemonade:
Make a full pitcher of lemonade and then save half of it in another pitcher. Add another favorite juice flavor, such as raspberry, strawberry-kiwi, white grape, peach, or something tropical with bananas, pineapple, and/or mango. Always add a slice or chunk of the secondary fruit as a garnish, either at the bottom of the glass, balanced on the rim, or frozen in an ice cube, to identify your newest beverage creation.

occasion as memorable, especially if you hire a pastry chef to come to the party to surprise the guest of honor with the presentation.

Vera Crawford of Steamboat Springs, Colorado, suggests hosting a croquet party on the summer solstice. Encourage guests to dress in old-fashioned summer clothing and big frilly hats. Serve lemonade, sandwiches, and little cakes.

For the children and some of the big kids in the group, create a full-sized maze with cardboard boxes and let them spend the afternoon trying to find their way out of it.

Devil's food cake, so rich and delicious that it must be sinful to eat, made its appearance in the American dessert case between 1900 and 1905. This decadent chocolate cake, a parallel to the popular, white angel food cake (circa 1870s), which was originally conceived as a way to use up surplus egg whites, quickly won the contest for long-lasting favor and flavor.

Host a "Just Dessert" party to meet the neighbors. Ask them to bring a classic dessert or a delectable treat of their own creation.

Renaissance Banquet

If you are interested in recreating the fourteenth century in your own backyard or inside your house, my advice is to first attend a Renaissance Faire and borrow, adopt, and outright steal ideas for what to serve on the menu, possible costume and entertainment options, and party game ideas. Nothing sets the stage faster for a celebration than music, so venture off to your local music store and search for any selection with Celtic, Irish, or Scottish overtones.

At the entrance to your banquet, provide costume pieces such as knight's helmets, boots,

The word *banquet* dates back to the fourteenth century and is from the Italian word *banchetto,* the small bench guests sit on during the feast.

swords, velvet capes, robes, flower garlands, and royal scepters and crowns. Call a party rental place to secure a wardrobe or hire a few of your handy friends to whip up the creations while you provide the fabric, fake jewels, and fabric glue. A visit to a second-hand store usually turns up a few items to be added to the wardrobe chest, and lastly, the local theater or the town's high school or college visual-art departments might be able to help with props to set the ambiance for such a festival.

To be authentic, the food must be all finger food, my good lady. Dining utensils, short of knives, were not used, and authenticity is key to a successful Renaissance dinner party. Soup is to be slurped, so do not provide spoons. Provide a basket of loaves of fresh-baked bread to be torn and passed along to the next guest (hence the expression "breaking the daily bread"). Instruct your guests to use the bread to soak up the remaining broth or to

Renaissance Activities: You can probably find many of these characters within your own group of friends:
- Set up a fortune teller's booth and table. Provide the crystal ball.
- Create a Shakespearean theater. Give the actors lines from a play and provide the audience with produce to throw if the actors perform badly.
- Comedy hour—recruit a jester to tell bad jokes.
- Host a jousting tournament and rally together any available knights in shining armor.

Fresh Rose Finger Bowl
   6 cups water
   6 drops essential rose oil
   6 small, freshly picked rose buds
Boil the water. After removing the water from the heat, add the essential oil. Stir gently to release the aroma and let the fragrant water cool. Fill each finger bowl with about 1/3 cup of the fragrant rosewater. Before the guests arrive, add a small, fresh rose bud to each.

Or match an essential oil with a slice of citrus—lemon, grapefruit, lime, or orange—to create different interpretations of a fragrant finger bowl.

scoop up any vegetables stuck at the bottom of the bowl or along the sides. The main course of turkey legs is also to be eaten without utensils. (Chicken legs or buffalo wings can be substituted if you expect a crowd.)

Napkins did not come into vogue nor were even considered a necessity until after the invention of the tablecloth. The Celts wiped their hands on bales of hay, which also served as the dining-room chairs in these days. Spartan hostesses placed a piece of soft bread beside each guest's dinner plate to be used as a napkin.

When serving messy finger foods, it is lovely to give your guests something better to clean their hands with than flimsy paper or cloth napkins. Borrow a tradition from Victorian days and offer each of your guests a refreshing finger bowl.

Encourage the children and any artists in the group to make shining armor for the knights who are scheduled to compete. Buy several rolls of aluminum foil and provide cardboard. The jousting stick can be made out of whatever stick is in the garage, which, when wrapped in foil and decorated with long strips of fabric, will resemble the artifact from centuries ago. Instead of real horses, elect the muscle-bound men of the crowd to charge, carrying a child. Divide the crowd in half to cheer for either the Red Knight or the Blue Knight, giving points to whoever stays upright the longest.

Sushi Parties

Dr. David and Nicole Guyot of Coto de Caza, California

Before my family moved away from the Pacific Ocean, close friends of ours hosted a sushi party. It is still talked about today by those who attended.

Pickled ginger (pink sushoga or red benishoga) is served with sushi to aid in digestion and provide an antidote to the raw fish.

First word of advice: invite a surgeon or dentist and hand over the sharp knives to this newly-elected sushi chef.

Secondly, only invite those who love sushi or are willing to give it a try.

Use calligraphy on your invitations to set the expectations for the party. Ideally, plan to roll and serve the sushi in an outdoor setting since there is little requirement of a kitchen and its usual utensils. Have those interested in learning how to make sushi step up to the sushi counter. If you have never made sushi before, you can always invite someone who has, hire a sushi chef, or wing it with the help of a cookbook propped up beside the eager students.

Borrow from a neighbor or friend to boost your inventory of Oriental dishes, cups, and teapots instead of purchasing new. String up paper lanterns and set the table with bamboo place mats and, of course, chopsticks.

While waiting for the edible works of art to be created, serve miso soup or a small green salad with ginger and soy dressing. Play new world music such as *Asian Groove*.

Conclude the meal with a few slices of juicy orange and maybe a small scoop of green-tea ice cream, an almond cookie, and green tea.

Shorts Party

Barbie Alman of Sebastopol, California.

At this much-anticipated annual summertime event, everyone is expected to wear decorated shorts—and they do. For example, an artist painted his shorts to look like a beach with the sun, palm trees, and seashells, and named them his "seashorts."

A carpenter made "board shorts" out of boards nailed together. They fit stiffly, were held up by suspenders, and were adorned with pliers, hammers, and screwdrivers.

The "cellulite shorts" couple arrived wearing pantyhose stuffed with bubble wrap under a pair of gigantic shorts. As you can only imagine, anything goes—encourage your crowd to borrow this fun party concept and design your own creative "shorts."

Olympic-Sized Party

This summer, host your own Olympics party. Invite the "teams" to dress in the colors of the country of their (dominant) origin and bring a sign or flag declaring what country they represent. Set up free-wheeling competitions, such as an obstacle course, car-tire shuffle, rope climb, long jump, disc throw (substitute a softball)—whatever you have readily available in your garage—to put together a crazy afternoon filled with smiles and laughs. Assign a staff photographer to be on standby for candid shots.

> *Gingerbread Houses:* This kid-friendly, finger-licking activity will keep the kids occupied for at least an hour and maybe some of the adults, too. Suggested ingredients: graham crackers, small Tootsie Rolls, peppermint sticks, black licorice, Hershey Kisses, and icing in tubes for ease of construction.

Christmas in July

In the middle of July, string a line or two of colored lights to add a glow to this festive party. Decorate a makeshift tree and hang ornaments from any tree or branch. Let your kids loose on this assignment about a week ahead of time.

On the invitations indicate that a dress code requires all guests to wear red, green, and white or at least one smidge of holiday color. Provide Santa hats or Rudolph's red nose (a clown nose does the trick) as party favors, and give them to your guests as they arrive. Be sure to rent a Santa suit to surprise the kids. Put on Christmas music and play it loud. Bake cookies together and eat them while they are still hot from the oven.

Let the white-elephant gift exchange be the pinnacle of the evening. Each guest will need to bring a wrapped gift (either something from home in working condition or purchased for less than five dollars). The first guest to arrive gets the number-one ticket and so on. The second person can choose a new gift or is permitted to take the already opened gift, which allows the first person to select again. The only rule is that a gift can change hands no more than three times. After the third time the gift changes hands, it stays with the recipient. The game continues until all of the gifts have been opened. You will be amazed at what some people want desperately.

Marie Antoinette Cake Party

When my business partner and I opened our advertising agency in Newport Beach, California, we were short of funds, but big on ideas for our open house. We adopted the idea from Marie Antoinette's infamous line at Versailles: "Let them eat cake."

Our office-warming party packed the place. Brian, the drawing talent of the partnership, whipped up a scene out of revolutionary France, complete with the gallows, a frenzied crowd, and an opening to place your head. Our guests took home Polaroids of themselves in the hot seat.

Around the conference-room table, various levels of cake plates and stands offered delectable slices of every type and flavor imaginable. Add your own twist to this idea. Encourage your friends to dress in period clothing and powdered white wigs, or rent costumes so they can dress upon arrival.

Everything Parisian

Dying to get out of the country to see the world and the worldly? Why not host a theme party with everything French. From

> The movie soundtrack to *Amelie* will put you immediately walking along the Seine.

the wine to the mustard to the bread, main meal, and dessert—you and your armchair travel buddies can make a vacation out of this *fête*. Suggest books to read all about Provence, and practice your French: *bon jour, croissant, au revoir.*

Give prizes for the tackiest-dressed American tourist, the most chic couple, and the best impersonation of famous French characters—royalty, actors, writers, artists, politicians, and chefs. For a roaring good time, parade the entrants by and let the entire party do the voting.

Tacky Tie Party

An old-time steakhouse in Trabuco Canyons located at the base of Saddleback Mountain in Southern California is known for whacking the ties off anyone who dares to wear one into the place. By the looks of the restaurant's walls and ceiling, many knew this was the place to get rid of their husband's ugliest ties.

For your steak-and-potatoes dinner, send invitations branded with your "ranch's" initials and the suggestion for everyone to wear the tackiest tie possible. At the door, greet your guests by cutting off the bottom half of their tacky ties and hanging for all to see. Give them a permanent marker to autograph their entry and date its year of birth, too. Allow the guests to vote for which is the worst tie.

Vinyl and Vino

Greg and Nancy Silver of Mission Viejo, California

At this party, you get to travel back through time with the aid of music. Ask guests to bring their favorite vinyl LP (as in long playing album, their 45s and 33 1/2 records) along with a bottle of their favorite *vino*. The challenge may be finding a turntable in operational condition. Open a bottle, play a song, and see how many titles and artists the group can identify. If you want to liven up the party, make it a contest between teams. Good wine and good music make for a good party.

> **It is only the first bottle that is expensive.**
> —*French proverb*

> **First flowers on the table, then food.**
> —*Danish proverb*

International Buffet

Do you know your neighbors' backgrounds? How about your good friends' heritages? Find out by hosting an international-buffet party, where each participant brings a specialty representing their heritage. Request that each chef identify his or her dish with the appropriate nation's flag. (You can supply them; visit your local party store or ask a young artist in the house to draw or print flags from the Internet and tape to toothpicks.) With family secrets shared by all, this worldly event could become an annual event. Make sure that you have a representative sampling of world music to get the crowd dancing.

The Easiest-Dish-Ever Party

At this party, the name of the game is to share the recipe of what you think is the easiest dish to prepare. Bring the dish and a copy of the recipe for everyone. At the bottom of it, type up a shopping list so the bottom can be cut off and slipped into a coupon holder or wallet. Be sure to put your name and number so that your friends can call and confirm what you already knew—"This is the easiest, greatest dinner ever!"

> In the southern states of America, the gardenia represents hospitality, the grace of southern living. In New Orleans's French Quarter, its fragrant blossoms perfume the air.

> **I drink to the general joy of the whole table.**
> —*William Shakespeare*
> *(c. 1564–1616)*

Accolades

Sometimes someone does an exceptional job or goes out of his or her way to help you. While a thank-you note is appropriate, it may not feel like quite enough.

Hostess Gifts

When someone takes the time and energy to host a party, it is a nice

Cooking and Dipping Oils:
Save your fancy oil and salad-dressing bottles. Wash and rinse thoroughly. Fill with the desired oil and add a spice: red chili pepper, a clove of (peeled) garlic, a few black and white peppercorns, or a sprig of thyme or rosemary.

To create a morning version of the same gift, add one or two vanilla beans, a cinnamon stick, or a stem of lavender in sweet almond, grapeseed, or walnut oil. With a handwritten tag tied around the bottle's neck, identify the flavor and suggest possible cooking applications.

gesture of appreciation to bring a hostess gift. Peruse the following list of much-appreciated gifts to find the perfect one for the perennial party thrower that you know.

Aromatic Dipping Oils: Deliver with a loaf of bread for an easy dinner tomorrow night.

Picnic Basket: Load with seasonal fruit and place an invitation inside to suggest a picnic later in the year.

Fruit Bowl: Fill with tiny votive candles, linen napkins, or napkins rings. Add a note complimenting the hostess on her wonderful parties.

Wooden or Metal Skewers: Wrap up with a fancy ribbon and a bottle of gourmet barbeque sauce.

Herbes de Provence: This attractive ceramic pot will look good on her counter and come in handy for future parties.

Cheese Tools: Present a boxed collection of cheese knives and spreaders.

Loose-Leaf Tea, Jams, and Jellies: Deliver with crumpets, muffins, or bagels for the next morning's breakfast.

Candle Snuffer and Decorative Matchboxes: Add a few tapers to complete the ensemble.

Gourmet Foods: Imported mustards, custards, or chocolates.

Party Dishes: Olive trays, salsa bowl, or nut dish with a jar or container to fill the dish.

Hostess Gift Idea submitted by Julie Hawkins of Costa Rica, Central America

Sugared Curried Pecans

1 lb pecan halves

1 egg white

¾ cup sugar

1½ tsp. curry powder

1 tsp. salt

Heat oven to 250° Fahrenheit. Lightly coat cookie sheet with vegetable cooking spray and arrange pecans in an even layer. Toast in oven, stirring occasionally, for about ten minutes. In a large bowl, whisk egg white and 1 teaspoon of water until frothy. Stir in toasted pecans and sprinkle with sugar, curry, and salt. Mix well. Return to greased cookie sheet and bake in a single layer for one hour, stirring once or twice.

Remember, the party does not have to be elaborate, grand, or expensive—it is the thought that counts. Practice simplicity in your party planning and watch how far your goodwill goes.

> You are the same today that you are going to be five years from now except for two things: the people with whom you associate and the books you read.
>
> —*Charles E. Jones (b. 1927)*

> We may live without friends,
> We may live without books,
> but civilized man cannot live without cooks.
>
> —*Meredith Owen (1831–1891)*

RESOURCES

* recommended reading

> No one who cooks, cooks alone. Even at her most solitary, a cook in the kitchen is surrounded by generations of cooks past, the advice and menus of cooks present, the wisdom of cookbook writers.
>
> —*Laurie Colwin (1944–1992)*

Peruse these many worthwhile reads about celebrating, food, and eating. Enjoy!

Different Dishes

Amuse~Bouche: Little Bites of Delight before the Meal Begins by Rick Tramonto and Mary Goodbody

At Home with Friends by Michele Adams and Gia Russo

Back to the Table: The Reunion of Food & Family by Art Smith

Bowl Food: Comfort Food for People on the Move by Laurel Glen

Emeril's New New Orleans by Emeril Lagasse

Heaven's Banquet: Vegetarian Cooking for Lifelong Health the Ayurveda Way by Miriam Kasin Hospodar

Intercourses: An Aphrodisiac Cookbook by Martha Hopkins and Randall Lockridge

Live, Love, Eat! The Best of Wolfgang Puck by Wolfgang Puck

Mollie Katzen's Sunlight Café by Mollie Katzen

My Kitchen in Spain by Janet Mendel

Nancy Silverton's Sandwich Book: The Best Sandwiches Ever—from Thursday Nights at Campanile by Nancy Silverton, Teri Gelber, and Amy Neunsinger

The Ayuredic Cookbook by Amadea Morningstar with Urmila Desai

The Chopra Center Cookbook: Nourishing Body and Soul by Deepak Chopra, David Simon, and Leanne Backer

The Frugal Gourmet Keeps the Feast: Past, Present and Future by Jeff Smith

The Japanese Kitchen by Hiroko Shimbo-Beitchman

The New Vegetarian Epicure by Anna Thomas

The Quick and Easy Ayurvedic Cookbook by Eileen Keavy Smith

> **A house without books is like a room without windows.**
> —Horace Mann (1796–1859)

More Party Ideas

Dinner after Dark: Sexy, Sumptuous Supper Soirées by Colin Cowie

Sheer Indulgences by John Hadamuscin

Susie Coehlo's Everyday Styling by Susie Coehlo

Viva la Vida: Festive Recipes for Entertaining Latin-Style by Rafael Palomino and Arlen Gargagliano

All about Ambiance

Preston Bailey's Design for Entertaining: Inspiration for Creating the Party of Your Dreams by Preston Bailey

Second Homes by Chippy Irvine

Tabletops: Easy, Practical, Beautiful Ways to Decorate the Table by Barbara Milo Ohrbach

Vastu Living: Creating a Home for the Soul by Kathleen Cox

Chocolate

Death by Chocolate: The Last Word on a Consuming Passion by Marcel Desaulniers

Why Women Need Chocolate: Eat What You Crave to Look Good and Feel Great by Debra Waterhouse

In Celebration of Women

Babyhood by Paul Reiser

Food & Mood: The Complete Guide to Eating Well and Feeling Your Best by Elizabeth Somer and Nancy L. Snyderman

Pregnant Women's Comfort Book: Self-Nurturing Guide to Your Emotional Well-Being During Pregnancy and Early Motherhood by Jennifer Louden

The Spirit of Pregnancy: An Interactive Anthology for Your Journey to Motherhood by Bonni Goldberg

To Your Health

Chai: The Spice Tea of India by Diana Rosen

Book of Green Tea by Christine Dattner

Healing Tonics by Jeanine Pollak

Herbal Teas: 101 Nourishing Blends for Daily Health and Vitality by Kathleen Brown

Scrumptious Tales

American Pie: Slices of Life (and Pie) from America's Back Roads by Pascale Le Draoulec

Aphrodite: A Memoir of the Senses by Isabel Allende

Encore Provence, New Adventures in the South of France (Vintage Departures) by Peter Mayle

Like Water for Chocolate by Laura Esquivel

Living La Dolce Vita: Bring the Passion, Laughter, and Serenity of Italy into Your Daily Life by Raeleen D'Agostino Mautner

A Moveable Feast by Ernest Hemingway

My Kitchen Wars by Betty Harper Fussell

Temptations: Igniting the Pleasures and Power of Aphrodisiacs by Ellen and Michael Alberston

The Mistress of Spices by Chitra Banerjee Divakaruni

The Unprejudiced Palate by Angelo Pellegrini

About the Author

Jill Murphy Long was born in 1963 and the party has not stopped since, thanks mainly to her mother's impromptu celebrations throughout the year—in addition to regularly scheduled birthdays and holidays. From blueberry picking in the Seven Mountains of Pennsylvania to nighttime ice-skating parties with bonfires on the frozen lakes of the Poconos to neighborhood treasure hunts (complete with a buried treasure chest), growing up in Jill's house meant putting on party shoes frequently.

This family tradition, handed down from mother to eldest daughter, continues strongly two decades later. More often than not, the author's family capitulates to her whims of bringing home a crowd for a barbeque, hosting a progressive-dinner party, or turning the garage into a spook-haunted alley in less than a day.

Jill has crisscrossed the United States both as a hungry traveler and restless resident of several states, sampling local cuisine at back-road diners, picking fresh ingredients from America's gardens and orchards, and borrowing recipes and regional traditions to create new recipes, party themes, and decorating ideas.

For more great party themes, truly easy recipes, and wild celebration ideas, visit her website at: www.permissionbooks.com.

Long is a former advertising executive, a working mother, a certified yoga instructor, and a professional writer. She is the author of *Permission to Nap* and *Permission to Play*. She lives in Steamboat Springs, Colorado, with her husband and daughter.